The
Enneagram
in Love

The Enneagram in Love

A ROADMAP FOR BUILDING AND STRENGTHENING ROMANTIC RELATIONSHIPS

Stephanie Barron Hall

ROCKRIDGE
PRESS

Interior and Cover Designer: Carlos Esparza
Art Producer: Tom Hood
Editors: Vanessa Ta and Nora Spiegel
Production Editor: Ruth Sakata Corley

Author photo courtesy of Brandon Hall

ISBN: Print 978-1-64611-941-7 | eBook 978-1-64611-942-4
R0

To Brandon, whose endless love, encouragement, and coffee have made this book possible. And to my parents, who have cheered me on in all my ventures.

CONTENTS

INTRODUCTION

The Enneagram has more pop culture buzz than ever, and this book aims to help seasoned students and newcomers to the Enneagram understand the self and others better. Whether you want to work on a relationship, or your partner handed you this book with a gentle nudge and dog-eared pages, I hope you find it useful.

As you read, it's natural to wonder where things have gone awry in your relationship, or plan your future successes. However, I first encourage you to sit with who you—and your partner—are right now. Notice things that you appreciate about each other and give voice to them. This will support your growth.

If a loved one gave you this book, you're in good company. My husband, Brandon, knew my fascination with personality typology and introduced me to the Enneagram. I had other interests at the time, and I found the complexity intimidating at first, so I brushed it off. Months later, my sister, Haley, also encouraged me to pick up the Enneagram. Like many good things in life, the second nudge was the one I needed.

I started by taking a free test online—although you'll learn that I don't recommend this method—and when the word "Achiever" popped up on the page I thought, "YES! I WON!" I had won the Enneagram test, and I was elated! As I learned more, this joy faded to a deep sadness and disorientation about my identity. I soon learned that Enneagram wisdom has a way of illuminating our darkest shadows, and only when we see ourselves clearly can we begin the process of growth. Self-acceptance, of course, is the first step. We can't change what we can't see, and we can't see when we get defensive, even toward ourselves. Thus began my journey of processing my identity, seeing beneath the exterior of who I believed I was, and finding steps toward growth.

As my husband and I navigated the Enneagram, we learned more about ourselves. As a type Three, I learned that when I feel things, I often feel discomfort, or an inner "ickiness," before emotion. When that feeling crept in before, I turned up the radio or jumped into a new project. Through the Enneagram, I've learned to tune into what I'm feeling, rather than avoid it with activity.

Brandon and I don't share an Enneagram type, but we do share the tendency to avoid our feelings. We didn't know this before; we thought everyone was like us, leaping from project to project, filling a calendar with exciting endeavors. We didn't realize that these were coping mechanisms used to outrun that creeping shame, sadness, anger, or fear that was always at our heels.

We've used the Enneagram to learn to acknowledge our feelings. We take time to process emotions together now, to give each other space to feel, and to ask good questions so that we can find the connection we've both always wanted but weren't sure how to find.

I hope that as you read and connect with your loved one, you'll find that connection, too. As you examine and strengthen your relationship through the wisdom of the Enneagram, you'll also find clarity, kindness, beauty, and love. In the following pages, I will first give an overview of the Enneagram: its origins, uses, and the information you need to find your type. Next, I'll explain how each of the types shows up in intimate relationships, including in the bedroom. Finally, I'll cover each of the 45 type pairings so that you can understand your partnership with greater clarity.

As you begin, I encourage you to be open to what you might learn: stay curious, practice gratitude, and expect transformation. Now let's get started.

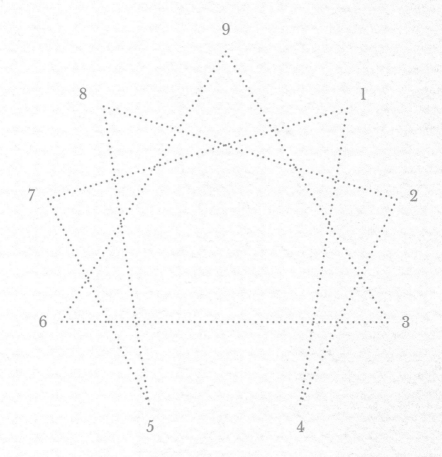

The Enneagram

The Enneagram is a motivation-based personality system oriented around nine core motivations. This focus on motivation requires that students cultivate greater self-understanding to truly understand and use the tool well. The beauty of the Enneagram is in its complexity. While not an exhaustive guide, this section is intended to offer a working understanding of what the Enneagram is and how to use it.

The Enneagram is often misunderstood as just another way to sort ourselves into boxes. In reality, the Enneagram is unique in that it is intended to act as a guide toward inner growth and change. Rather than simply describing us, like many other personality profiling systems do, the Enneagram is intended to uncover underlying motivations so that we can move from our personality "box" and into greater integration and wholeness. It sheds light on the parts of ourselves we're unaware of or don't want to admit, and it helps us understand how to move toward health according to our specific type. We often live on autopilot, but understanding the Enneagram helps us to see ourselves and our way of being in the world more clearly so that we can live with more intention.

A BRIEF HISTORY

The modern Enneagram is an interwoven system of ancient wisdom and contemporary psychology. While its exact origins are unknown, its most notable contributors are George Gurdjieff, Oscar Ichazo, and Claudio Naranjo (Riso & Hudson, 1999).

"Enneagram" means nine-sided (ennea) drawing (gram), and the shape itself dates back millennia (Riso & Hudson, 1999). George Gurdjieff began teaching his version of the tool in the early 1900s, having been led to the Enneagram symbol through his studies of religious, philosophical, and other oral traditions. Gurdjieff is primarily known for using the Enneagram shape and all its symbolism to guide his students toward enlightenment (Chestnut, 2013).

Like the Enneagram symbol, the nine personality archetypes also have ancient roots, but Oscar Ichazo developed them further (Chestnut, 2013). The modern Enneagram emerged when Ichazo combined Gurdjieff's work with further developments in his own study of the human psyche. Ichazo identified nine "ego fixations" in his studies, based on the seven deadly sins, plus deceit and fear (Riso & Hudson, 1999). He combined these nine core motivations with the Enneagram symbol to form the nine types as we know them.

Ichazo overlaid his discovery over Gurdjieff's work, called "The Fourth Way" (Chestnut, 2013), to establish what we now call the Enneagram (Riso & Hudson, 1999). Once Ichazo's work gained traction, he imparted much of this wisdom to California

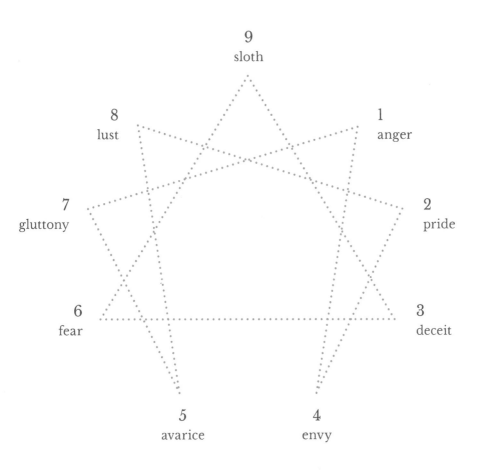

psychiatrist Claudio Naranjo. Naranjo then emerged as one of the founders of the present Enneagram of personality (Chestnut, 2013).

Many important texts from Enneagram scholars were written in the 1980s by Jesuits, spiritual seekers, psychiatrists, and professors, among others. Specifically, Father Richard Rohr, spiritual directors, and even Mother Teresa used the Enneagram for their own spiritual development (Heuertz, 2017). However, these works affected only a small segment of people, and the Enneagram didn't gain broad appeal until its reemergence in the 2000s. Since then, a growing number of people have found it to be a useful framework for growth. For the past 40 years or so, the Enneagram has been used broadly in Christian contexts, though no present-day religious entity can lay claim to the tool or its wisdom.

The early developers of the modern Enneagram found that each of us has a set of coping and defense mechanisms, stories, patterns, and motivations that create our personality. Many personality typologies stop there, but the Enneagram helps us uncover the true essence—hidden deep within the self—of what it means to be who we truly are. As Riso and Hudson write, "The Enneagram does not put us in a box, it shows us the box we are already in—and the way out."

The personality is our default operating mode, but as we study the Enneagram, we can observe our standard ways of interacting and choose a more self-supportive, helpful way of being. The path to self-improvement begins with this self-awareness—you cannot change what you do not know exists.

Studying the Enneagram guides growth by drawing attention to the unchallenged patterns in our personality. Observing and giving voice to these patterns helps us see the ways that we are selling ourselves short or stunting growth by staying within our normal frame of mind. Uncovering our core motivation draws attention to our shadow side, or those parts of the self that we subconsciously know exist but would rather not see. The shadows are the darkest parts of ourselves. We typically hide from or numb them, but this severely hinders our growth. The Enneagram brings the shadows into the light so that we can find growth, and it also highlights our strengths.

The Enneagram's impact on relationships and communication is one of the best reasons I've found to study it. The simple realization that we are all different is enough to help us extend more empathy and compassion to others. Understanding our partner's Enneagram type helps us understand them a bit better, so we can offer kindness when our wires get crossed. The Enneagram gives us a common language to discuss challenges and insights, and acts as a guide to a closer, more fulfilling relationship.

The Intelligence Centers

The Enneagram can be broken down into three Centers of Intelligence: Heart (2, 3, 4), Head (5, 6, 7), and Gut (or Body) (8, 9, 1). This powerful component acknowledges views of intelligence beyond "book smarts," which are typically most prized in many Western cultures. The Enneagram encourages each type to harness the power of their own Center of Intelligence.

Head types perceive through thinking. Each of the Head types has a go-to thought mechanism for warding off their underlying fear and anxiety.

Fives learn all they can because they believe knowledge and competence will keep them from being overwhelmed by the world outside their minds. Sixes plan for the worst-case scenario because they believe that planning and preparation will keep them safe and secure. Sevens run headlong into the future because they believe they can avoid feeling anxious by holding tightly to freedom and opportunity.

The Gut or Body types perceive through gut intuition. Each of the Gut types has a tactic to cope with the anger bubbling inside them.

Eights confront their anger head-on and are the most outwardly "angry" of this triad. Nines fall asleep to their anger to keep the peace and may not even know it exists. Ones repress their anger because it is not appropriate, although it then leaks out as resentment.

The Heart types perceive through emotional intelligence. Each of the Heart types have a particular way of dealing with their deep shame as they search for their true identity.

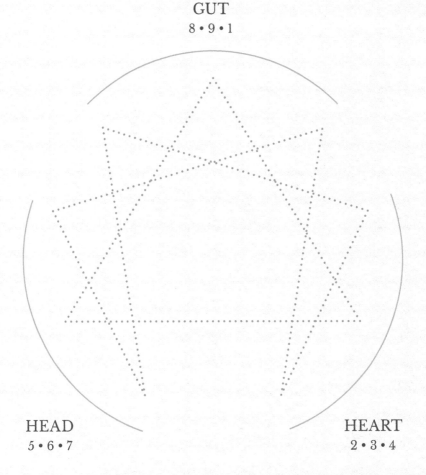

GUT

8 • 9 • 1

HEAD

5 • 6 • 7

HEART

2 • 3 • 4

Twos are keenly attuned to the feelings of others and often feel what those around them are feeling. They are often more connected to the feelings of others than they are to their own. Threes create a self-image of worth through productivity. Their shame pushes them toward their picture of success. Fours are deeply introspective and explore their feelings internally. They search to find their own true identity as they feel they need a deeper connection with their true selves.

WHAT'S YOUR TYPE?

Terms like *self-care*, *self-love*, and *self-improvement* saturate our culture. This fascination with personal development includes fascination with the personality and personality assessments. Most people like to learn about themselves, and this self-awareness from diving deeply into personality analysis encourages our growth. There are dozens of ways to measure personality, but the Enneagram is popular for its eerie accuracy and dynamic complexity.

Many Enneagram enthusiasts describe their first encounter with their type as a deeply resonant experience. Reading the thoughts and motivations buried deep within can unsettle and comfort us simultaneously. Exposing the true self can be unnerving, but knowing others experience life similarly can be reassuring.

The self-understanding that Enneagram wisdom offers does not materialize overnight; it unfolds gradually. I find that tests can be counterproductive for this reason. Rather than relying upon a quick online test for a black-and-white answer, I recommend self-reflection, contemplation, and self-discovery to find your type.

To find your type:

BEGIN WITH CURIOSITY. Withholding self-judgment is one of the most important elements of self-observation. While slipping into self-criticism is tempting—especially when reading about the negative traits of each Enneagram type—it is neither helpful nor productive. I recommend cultivating curiosity instead. Rather than thinking, "I hate that I do that," try "Huh, that's an interesting response. I wonder why I do that."

The Enneagram is ultimately about uncovering the unconscious patterns and stories we've carried inside us throughout life, and the self-compassion in the latter reaction helps you to see yourself more clearly.

While tests provide a specific path to find your type, I recommend holding the results loosely. Tests can diminish the value of learning about yourself as you try to determine your type, and the results can confuse a new Enneagram student. The slow route is better.

FOCUS ON MOTIVATION, NOT BEHAVIOR. This specific correction will pop up time and again in Enneagram study. It is much easier to judge a person's outer appearance and behavior, but the real work is in understanding motivation. It's important to keep in mind what truly motivates you when considering type descriptions. For example, sometimes Threes and Fives exhibit similar behavior. They both love to learn, for instance, but their deeply held motivations for engaging in that behavior are quite different. Pay attention to the motivation of each type as you learn.

Many Enneagram tests are inaccurate because they focus on behavior and fail to adequately assess core motivation. Typically, the only tests I recommend are the iEQ9 and the EnneaApp (see page 184). Even with these tests, it's important to hold the results loosely in your mind. The process of discovering your Enneagram type is ultimately an exercise in learning to trust yourself: as you learn, observe, study, and reflect, remember that at the end of it all, it's your type. Only YOU know your core motivation. You can trust yourself to uncover it.

You'll find a discussion of each Enneagram type and some important educational information surrounding Enneagram theory in the next sections. They will be useful as you and your partner learn more about the Enneagram together. A discussion of the Enneagram types in love will follow, and the book will conclude with detailed descriptions of all 45 type pairings. This material is intended to help you understand yourself and your partner more clearly, so you can cultivate the fulfilling, connected relationship you desire. While it's tempting to tell your partner what type they are, consider handing them the book to read for themselves. They may find themselves with more certainty when they're able to approach it with fresh eyes.

Basic Personality Type

It's common to see yourself in several of the personality type descriptions as you read. Taking time to journal, reflect, or ponder your core motivations can be helpful. Get curious and ask yourself why you do what you do. Consider your response to this question, then ask again. When you have asked "Why?" five or six times, you'll likely get closer to your core motivation. Remember that this type of self-discovery is not instant, and it can take more time than expected to identify your type. If you can't figure it out in this opening section, read on for more clarity. Sometimes we can see ourselves most clearly when we read how we relate with others.

It will be helpful to return to the Intelligence Centers sidebar to consider your type. When self-typing, most people are able to choose a few types that resonate, and these are often in different Intelligence Centers. Returning to that section will be useful to see yourself more clearly.

The types are:

TYPE ONE | The Improver

TYPE TWO | The Helper

TYPE THREE | The Performer

TYPE FOUR | The Individualist

TYPE FIVE | The Observer

TYPE SIX | The Loyalist

TYPE SEVEN | The Enthusiast

TYPE EIGHT | The Challenger

TYPE NINE | The Peacemaker

Type One | The Improver

Type One is called the Improver. Ones are motivated by the need to be truly good and right. They believe an ideal world could exist, and they work hard to bring it into existence. As members of the Gut Intelligence Center, Ones have underlying anger that they feel is inappropriate to express. Instead, they turn their anger inward in the form of an inner critic—an incessant, berating voice that focuses on every area in which the One is falling short of perfection. Ones turn the harshest criticism inward, while outwardly, they are diligent, intentional, and purposeful. They are thoughtful and considerate of the needs of others, and they want to make the world a better place.

Type Two | The Helper

Type Two is called the Helper. Twos are motivated by the need to be loved and wanted, and they believe they are most lovable when they are helping others. They use their keen emotional intelligence to understand what others need, and offer constant support, encouragement, and love to the people around them. Twos genuinely want others to feel loved and satisfied, yet they often forget to take care of their own needs in the process. When unhealthy, Twos give love to others to get love in return. As members of the Heart center, Twos are emotionally aware, and they tend to reflect the feelings of others with great compassion.

Type Three | The Performer

Type Three is called the Performer. Threes are motivated by the need to find their worth and value in their productivity. Threes are high achievers and strive for success in whatever way most resonates with their cultural or familial upbringing. As members of the Heart center, they sense the emotional energy of a room and adapt to fit what they believe is expected of them. This chameleon-like quality allows Threes to connect easily with others, yet sometimes Threes aren't as aware of who they truly are. Threes stay busy to avoid feeling their feelings, and they are highly productive, engaging, and adaptable.

Type Four | The Individualist

Type Four is called the Individualist. Fours are motivated by the need to find their true heart. Fours tend to feel that they are different from others; sometimes they love being different, and sometimes they hate it. They long to be deeply seen and loved for who they are, yet they are on a lifelong quest to become more of whom they believe themselves to be. Fours are idealists who long for a world that is not reality, and they mourn the shortcomings they see. Fours are in the Heart center, and they feel all their feelings deeply. They are on a lifelong quest to find meaning and significance in their life, yet in their longing, they often miss the beauty that exists all around them.

Type Five | The Observer

Type Five is called the Observer. Fives are motivated by the need to be competent and self-sufficient. Fives only have a specific amount of energy for each day, so they conserve their energetic, emotional, and material resources to avoid feeling depleted. As members of the Head center, Fives aim to manage underlying fear and anxiety by collecting information they believe will calm them. Fives are cerebral and thoughtful, and they tend to be able to retain a vast amount of information, especially related to their niche interests.

Type Six | The Loyalist

Type Six is called the Loyalist. Sixes are motivated by the need to be supported and safe. Sixes often don't trust others easily, but once they do, they are deeply loyal and enduring. As members of the Head center, Sixes use worst-case scenario contingency planning to manage any fear or anxiety that might pop up when they consider what could go wrong. They make plans to ensure their survival, and they make sure the community is safe as well. Sixes tend to be friendly, analytical, and responsible. They are often the ones who make sure everything gets done.

Type Seven | The Enthusiast

Type Seven is called the Enthusiast. Sevens are motivated by the need to retain their freedom and escape pain or boredom. They are fun-loving adventure seekers who enjoy spreading laughter wherever they go. As members of the Head center, Sevens avoid their inner fear or anxiety by running headlong into the future, believing that if they are always moving, they'll never get trapped. Sevens see everything in life as an opportunity, yet they are often so busy planning the next adventure that they don't allow themselves to enjoy the moment. While they want others to share in their happiness, their independent streak sometimes causes them to leave others behind. Sevens are versatile, optimistic, and idealistic.

Type Eight | The Challenger

Type Eight is called the Challenger. Eights are motivated by the need to protect themselves from being controlled by others. Eights often get a reputation for being bullies, but this couldn't be further from the truth. Eights fight the injustice they see around them and will stand up for the vulnerable. They seek the truth, and they don't mind dismantling cultural norms to find it. As members of the Gut center, Eights are well-acquainted with their anger and don't mind confrontation. The Eight's larger-than-life energy can be intimidating or too intense for others, leaving others feeling bulldozed and the Eight feeling misunderstood.

Type Nine | The Peacemaker

Type Nine is called the Peacemaker. Nines are motivated by the need to be at peace both internally and externally, and to maintain unity and connection. Nines constantly feel trapped between two forces: the outside world of demands, pressure, and calls upon their energy, and the inside world of their thoughts, feelings, and opinions. Avoiding this pressure can cause Nines to mentally fall asleep to themselves. As members of the Gut center, Nines have an undercurrent of anger, but they often aren't aware of it since they spend so much time keeping the peace. Nines have only a limited amount of energy each day. They spend much of it keeping the peace, believing any disruption will break the connections they have built with others.

The Wing

Your core type does not change, as it is attached to your core motivation. The wing is an adjacent type to your core type, and alters your behavior. Your core type is the *why*, and your wings are the *how*. Most Enneagram scholars agree that wings can shift throughout life (Riso & Hudson, 1999). In my coaching and teaching, I have found that some people feel they have a strong wing, some people feel they have balanced wings, and some people don't have a wing at all.

You may have noticed that the side-by-side Enneagram types seem somewhat opposite. This is a component that makes the Enneagram so dynamic. The types on either side of our core type offer much needed balance and perspective. Type Two, for example, is highly relational, yet they have highly task-oriented types on either side. The wings bring balance to the core type.

It's useful to understand your wing(s), because specific wing and core type combinations can alter the way a type shows up in the world. For example, an Eight with a Nine wing is more calm, steady, and enduring than an Eight with a Seven wing, who is typically more gregarious, independent, and forceful. Wings are demarcated by a lowercase "w" between the core and wing type: COREwWING, or 8w7. When a person feels they have either both or no wings, they will typically drop the "w" altogether and simply write "8."

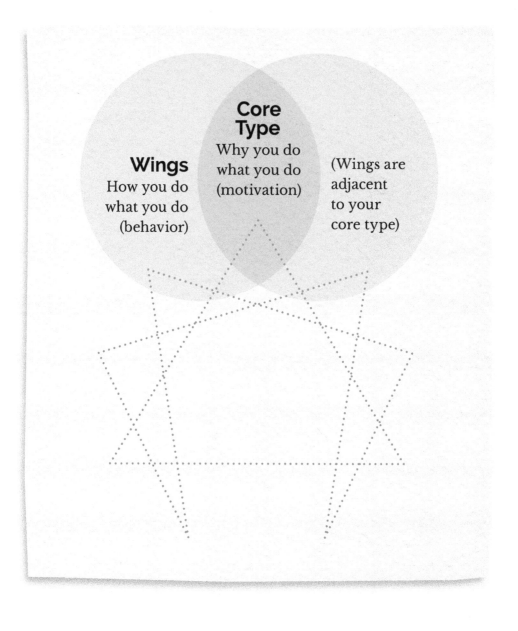

Core Type

Why you do what you do (motivation)

Wings

How you do what you do (behavior)

(Wings are adjacent to your core type)

USING THE ENNEAGRAM

You likely have a good idea by now about your own type, and you may even have a guess about your partner's type. The Enneagram offers much wisdom, but you must begin to do the hard work of growth to access it. Here are a few guidelines to get you started:

NOTICE YOUR TENDENCIES. The Enneagram calls attention to the hidden or subconscious patterns in our lives. Observing your patterns and their motivations beneath can jumpstart your growth process.

QUESTION YOUR PATTERNS. What responses no longer serve you? What do you believe about yourself that may not be true anymore? What patterns pop up time and again when you encounter stress or conflict? If your typical pattern is to react first and think later, consider pausing before you engage. If you are more likely to stay silent in conflict, practice speaking up for yourself when the stakes are low. The idea is not that our patterns are always wrong, but that when they have gone unchallenged for a lifetime, they may get in the way of our growth.

BEGIN TO TELL YOURSELF A NEW STORY. When we're on autopilot, our thoughts, feelings, and actions tend to get ahead of us. We tell ourselves stories about who we are and the way we engage with others. When you tell yourself a new story, you can find a new path toward wholeness.

ENGAGE EMPATHY AND COMPASSION. This journey is challenging, especially at first. As you become healthier, you will continually find new ways that you can grow. Throughout your Enneagram journey, a little empathy will go a long way. Take deep breaths, be kind to yourself, and be kind to your love.

You likely chose this book because you're looking for a more fulfilling, engaged connection with your partner. The Enneagram requires thought, feeling, and action to help you create the relationship you both desire. This journey requires that you show up with authenticity and honesty. Growth is often painful, but the transformation is worth it.

The next chapters will lay more groundwork for the final section. Section two will cover how each type shows up in a romantic relationship, and the inherent expectations of emotional vulnerability, communication, and connection therein. The third section will put it all together in detailed descriptions of each of the 45 relationship pairings, including strengths, areas to work on, and intimacy. The real work will happen here. As you read, be gentle with yourself and your partner, and use this knowledge as a path toward growth. These sections will help you strengthen your communication, deepen your connection, and find your way forward.

Levels of Development

This concept of "levels of development" was developed by Don Richard Riso and Russ Hudson to further illuminate the power of Enneagram work. In their studies, they identified three general levels of development: healthy, average, and unhealthy (Riso & Hudson, 1999). An individual can fluctuate greatly among these.

(Riso & Hudson, 1999)

It's harder to tell a person's type when they are very healthy. In this state, the ego self is no longer the main actor in their life, and the individual is living from the essence of who they are with true freedom, full self-awareness, and self-acceptance. In the average range, individuals begin to identify strongly with the stereotypical personality patterns of their type. Most of us are in the average range most of the time, and health can vary greatly even within this range. Those in the average range typically display some healthy and some unhealthy characteristics. In the unhealthy range, a person begins to believe that their strengths are actually the reason things are falling apart for them. For example, a Three might fall into believing that all of their efforts are in vain and can become despondent and self-sabotaging. Any type in this level becomes self-destructive and highly troubled.

All nine types can move along this growth continuum. Individuals of the same type can seem quite different when living in different levels of health.

LEVEL OF DEVELOPMENT	LOOKS LIKE
HEALTHY	True freedom
	Self-awareness
	Self-actualization
AVERAGE	Stereotypical
	Identification with personality patterns
	Interpersonal conflict
UNHEALTHY	"Rock bottom"
	Destructive beliefs & behavior
	Pathologies

(Riso & Hudson, 1999)

The Personality Types in Love

One of the most effective ways to use the Enneagram is in relationships. Romantic relationships can be beautiful, fulfilling, challenging, and lonely all at once. When I first learned the Enneagram, I could suddenly see beyond my own perspective, and all my relationships seemed clearer than ever. It felt like seeing the world in color for the first time. Communication with my husband eased. Talking about the Enneagram together diffused complicated conversations. We still have them, of course, but the Enneagram offers perspective that brings connection rather than division.

I encourage you to read these descriptions of each type in a romantic relationship with fresh empathy. Seeking greater understanding of yourself and your partner can simplify communication, release tension, and reinvigorate your love.

Each type will be described through the lens of health throughout this section. How each type shows up in relationships depends on whether their level of development is unhealthy, average, or healthy. Consider as you read that most stereotypical traits of each Enneagram type reflect the average level of health. As any type becomes healthier, they will look more balanced and less stereotypical.

Everyone experiences and expresses intimacy differently. Because intimacy is largely behavioral, and varies based on upbringing, subtype, and background, Enneagram type isn't always an accurate predictor of intimate relationships. I surveyed hundreds of individuals of various types when writing this section and found themes surrounding each type and their approach to the bedroom. Each type generally longs to cultivate both emotional intimacy and physical intimacy in a fulfilling relationship with their partner. The survey responses, combined with my Enneagram knowledge, have informed the thoughts on intimacy in this section.

ONE: THE IMPROVER

In a relationship, Ones are sincere, thoughtful, and conscientious. Ones tend to approach all of life with great intention and purpose, and the same is true in their relationships. Ones often seem very serious, and get a reputation for being rigid, but it's normally because they see all the details that need to be accomplished before they can rest. Deep down, Ones love to have fun, and they love a partner who can bring that out in them.

Ones are loyal and committed in romantic relationships. Consistency is important to them, both in their own lives and in romantic partnership. They appreciate someone they can depend on. Ones are typically focused on their self-improvement, and they want their sense of self and personal growth to be on an upward trajectory. They are similarly eager to grow in relationships—especially when the relationship is young—and they want to continually find deeper connection with their partner.

Levels of Development

Unhealthy Ones are self-righteous and dogmatic. They believe they know the truth and are the gatekeepers of what is right in life. They can be intolerant and inflexible, and highly judgmental of themselves and their partner. When very unhealthy, they can become obsessive about fixing everything they see.

In average levels of health, Ones are still aware of their inner critic, but they know that it is unkind and unacceptable to project that judgment onto others. As a result, they might find themselves caught in tension or rigidity because they are guided by a negative inner voice. Because Ones are generally prone to seek self-improvement, average Ones will look for ways to grow and refine themselves. They may have an inner struggle between who they want to be and who they currently are, yet they hold tight to their idealism and express the "right" morals for others to follow. Ones may not always be able to articulate what they feel, but they often would like to know, and would love their partner to help them wade into vulnerability. Especially in average health, Ones often feel the need to take on everything alone in their relationships, and they may feel like they are the only responsible adult in the room. This tendency can make them great partners, but it can also leave them feeling drained and resentful, and their partners can feel unduly criticized.

Healthy Ones are more realistic about the world. They see where they and their partner have fallen short, and they hold these downfalls in tension with all the beauty and good they see around them. They are ethical, principled, and balanced. They are incredibly attentive in their relationships and see every small detail of life as a piece of a bigger purpose. Healthy

Ones seek to find the good, the honorable, and the perfectly imperfect in themselves and their partner, rather than chasing elusive ideals of the less healthy levels. Their ideals drive them toward others, not away.

Communication & Conflict

Ones want their partner to be as honest and thoughtful as they are. Ones put thought behind every action and inaction, and they go to great lengths to choose the right way to respond, engage, and live. They expect the same thoughtfulness from their partner, and this can leave them feeling disappointed, especially when unhealthy. No one enjoys being lied to, but even a white lie can be a red flag for Ones. They prioritize honesty and integrity in themselves and their partner.

Ones tend to be idealists, so they are often able to see potential in relationships and opportunity for improvement both in their relationship and in their partner. Ones rarely give partial effort to an endeavor, and a romantic partnership is no different. If you are with a One, you can expect that they will be diligent in cultivating a good relationship.

Ones tend to prioritize remaining rational and calm in conflict. They may express frustration, but Ones tend to emphasize figuring things out, rather than getting caught in emotional entanglements. Partners who share this conflict style may both get quiet, pull back, or take space to think and problem solve.

This approach to conflict can feel challenging for the One's partner, because the One's lack of emotionality can cause the partner to feel that the One is not present in the conflict. The tendency toward calm problem-solving that is meant to resolve conflict more efficiently can actually cause greater misunderstanding. Ones can spend so much time remaining composed that they neglect to truly process emotions, so expect that Ones may need a little time to process feelings.

When they need space to process, Ones may consider saying something like, "I want you to know I'm present with you, and I'm feeling something, but I'm just not sure what yet." The Enneagram can offer a different perspective on a One's emotional detachment in conflict, helping us avoid frustration by reminding us that not everyone thinks the same way we do.

Intimacy

Various forms of intimacy are important for Ones to feel loved and known by their partner. They cultivate emotional intimacy in relationships through intentional and honest conversation, connection, and sharing their feelings. For many Ones, intimacy is built and deepened over time.

My research indicates that Ones approach sex in very different ways. Some Ones feel that they can't get out of their heads and want everything—including sex—to be planned, routinized, and structured. They often can't stop thinking about their to-do list and have an especially difficult time when they don't feel that their partner has shown up for them in practical ways throughout the day. For some Ones, it's hard to "turn it on" out of the blue; they need to build time and trust through interactions in and out of the bedroom.

On the other hand, many Ones find an opportunity for release from structure and control in sex. When surveyed, many Ones said they love to let their partner take control so they can relax. A spontaneous encounter may catch them off guard in a good way; they can get caught in the moment rather than feeling stuck in their head.

Many Ones find themselves attempting to be perfect: the perfect partner, lover, or date. This pressure can be crippling and prevent Ones from experiencing relationships and life to the fullest.

Ones need self-acceptance to engage intimately. A loving partner can speak louder than the One's inner critic at times, and this experience can be incredibly healing. Ones may need reassurance from a partner that they are good, right, and doing well. Lasting change, however, must often come from within. Enneagram work can be restorative for Ones, as they realize that their inner critic doesn't get the final say on their worth and value in the world. The ability to turn down the volume on this negative voice and turn up the loving messages will increase self-acceptance and intimacy and be healing for Ones in relationships.

Key Points

As a One, you likely see the possibility of an ideal world, and you feel it is your responsibility to create it. You may exhaust yourself attempting to fix everything around you and miss what is already good. Try making a list of things you are grateful for each day. Think about what you love about your partner and share that with them.

How we speak to ourselves is often how we speak to others, so your self-critical inner voice may at times project onto your partner. It's important to recognize this because you might feel you are trying to help, while your partner may feel criticized. Awareness of this dynamic can help create a more loving approach from both parties.

FOR THOSE IN A RELATIONSHIP WITH A ONE

If you're in a relationship with a One, let them know how much you appreciate them for all they do—be specific!—and let them know they can depend on you by taking responsibility. Consider becoming an expert in a few household chores that they can count on you to do, taking initiative and planning a thoughtful date, or supporting them in a specific task on their to-do list.

TWO: THE HELPER

In a relationship, Twos are benevolent, warm, passionate, and optimistic. Twos are highly empathetic, and sometimes feel the feelings of their partner rather than their own feelings, without realizing it. It's important for Twos to feel that they have space to process their own feelings, and they appreciate a partner who can draw that out of them. Underneath the Two's helpfulness and generosity is a deep desire to feel truly loved and wanted.

Twos put a lot of energy into their relationships. They are loving and intentional, and they truly give from the heart to their partner, so it's important that Twos feel their partner is also showing up, putting in effort, and making space for them. Twos feel most valued when their partner is present with them, especially in emotional conversation. Twos love to be drawn out and asked how they really feel, but sometimes it takes direct questions for them to share. Because Twos spend so much time focusing on others, they don't always spontaneously offer how they are feeling or thinking.

Levels of Development

Less healthy Twos become demanding about getting their needs met. They can be manipulative and use their emotional attunement to get what they want rather than to help others. In a romantic relationship, unhealthy Twos place such a high value on reciprocity that any little action on their part will require even greater repayment from their partner. They are not aware of how contentious and destructive their relationship is, or that their entire world revolves around perceived love or lack of it from their partner. Unhealthy Twos tend to lose themselves in relationships, as they find ways to conform completely to be whomever they believe their partner wants.

In average levels of health, Twos sometimes still give to get, but it's not nearly as pronounced. Deep down, they long to encourage, praise, and love others, especially their romantic partner. As much as Twos long to be fulfilled in their relationship, they want their partner to feel the same love, fulfillment, and support. Average Twos tend to engage in people-pleasing behavior, so they often read the emotional temperature of their partner and believe they must fix it. Their love leads them to seek a high level of intimacy, especially emotional intimacy and togetherness. A Two at this level of development, might absorb all negativity or stress from their partner and create a world where their partner can thrive, without realizing that they are neglecting their own well-being.

At their healthiest, Twos are truly altruistic. They give of themselves freely without any expectation of return, and they are inspiring, nurturing, and deeply loving. They know that their partner isn't theirs to fix, so they have a keen understanding of what emotional weight is theirs to carry and what belongs to their partner. Healthy Twos know that their relationship with self is as important as their relationship with their partner and that they cannot give when depleted.

Communication & Conflict

Twos want their partner to be as benevolent and warm as they are. They build deep connections with others, so Twos often love a partner who also likes to be connected with others outside the relationship.

Twos love to be asked good questions. In average levels of health they aren't always able to pinpoint their own emotions, so answering questions helps them untangle their real feelings. The reciprocity and help Twos both offer and seek is often based in a desire to know and love others, and for others to seek to know them.

Twos who are growing know they don't always have to say yes, but it's always helpful to remind them. Twos often extend themselves for others and reach out first, so they feel loved and cared for when others reach out first for a change.

In conflict, Twos may need reassurance that the relationship is not in jeopardy. Once that is established, they will be better able to be present in a difficult conversation. Twos are not fragile; they have great emotional strength, but they still need gentleness in conflict. When offering feedback to a Two in a relationship, it may be helpful to cushion the feedback with what you love and appreciate about them on either side of the challenging message.

Because Twos work hard to build a good relationship, it can be challenging for them when it is tumultuous. Twos will often try to stay positive, uplifting, and optimistic in conflict. This can cause their partner to feel at times like the Two is unwilling to be present in the conflict, and things may go unaddressed for longer than is helpful due to the Two's unwillingness to approach the topic. Twos tend to be expressive and fairly verbal overall, so the same is true in their relationships.

Understanding the Enneagram can help Twos realize that it's not a sign they aren't loved when their partner doesn't ask questions or isn't as present and attentive as they would like. Everyone should have a partner who shows up for them and is engaged in the relationship, but Twos sometimes want so much engagement that no amount of love feels like enough. Once Twos notice this tendency in themselves, they can be more aware of it and more forgiving when others don't meet their needs exactly as they had hoped.

Intimacy

Intimacy for Twos is about much more than physical closeness. Because they are so relational and attentive to their partners, emotional connection is a powerful form of intimacy. When surveyed, Twos shared that their emotional needs must be met for sex to be truly intimate.

Twos want to be close and needed, but they also care deeply about being loved and wanted. Emotional and physical intimacy make many Twos feel wanted, seen, and known. Long heart-to-hearts and deep conversation are critical to cultivate the loving intimacy they desire. Many Twos find that being fully open and honest with each other without judgment is a powerfully grounding experience in a partnership. Having an attentive partner in both conversation and the bedroom helps a Two feel connected.

Twos often give attention, love, and presence to their partner, so receiving the same in return can transform the relationship. Because Twos spend their energy encouraging others, being encouraged and genuinely complimented enhances their emotional connection. Twos prioritize intimacy—especially emotional intimacy—over other aspects of the relationship. Even if they don't feel they have deep agreements with their partner around various practical or theoretical topics, the relationship can feel fulfilling for Twos if they have deep emotional intimacy.

When emotional intimacy is lacking in a relationship, Twos can sometimes feel used by sexual intimacy. However, in my research, I heard from many Twos that their partner's sexual satisfaction often takes precedence over their own experience. Many Twos mentioned that they have a difficult time explaining to their partner what they like in the bedroom because their life has been so focused on pleasing others. If you're in a relationship with a Two, consider asking what they like. Take time to communicate and give them loving, judgment-free space to grow your connection.

Key Points

For a healthier relationship, begin to notice when you're giving to get versus when you are giving of yourself from a place of altruism. When you are feeling stretched too thin after extending yourself to help others, take a step back and consider what help you would offer to a friend in your position. How would you care for them? What might that feel like? Try offering yourself the same care you offer to others.

Twos can feel frustrated, lonely, and resentful when they don't feel seen or cared for by their partner. Twos give to others at times what they want others to give them, but they aren't as skilled at asking for what they need. If you feel resentment bubbling up, consider that your partner may not realize that your needs aren't being met. Try to be kind and clear about your needs, and look for the little ways that your partner is showing care and love, even if it's not the exact way you would like it.

Reciprocity is necessary in relationships, but high standards can lead to an imbalance. Practice accepting love, help, and kindness from your partner with deep appreciation. In love, keeping score rarely leads to happiness; practice an open-handed approach to reciprocity rather than insisting on even give-and-take.

FOR THOSE IN A RELATIONSHIP WITH A TWO

If you're in a relationship with a Two, you probably have experienced their incredible warmth, passion, and kindness. Offer the same generosity back by reaching out to them first, asking them questions about their day or their dreams, and making space for uninterrupted quality time. Learn how your Two feels most loved and do that for them whenever you get the chance. For some Twos, it's a back rub or a cup of coffee, and for others it's a heartfelt note or a deep conversation. Let them know how much you appreciate them for who they are and not just for what they do for you.

THREE: THE PERFORMER

When a Three sets their mind on something, they typically show up fully every step of the way and will approach any scenario with optimism and excellence. The same is true of their relationships. While they can get the reputation that they only care about getting ahead, this isn't necessarily the case. Threes are loving and kind in relationships. They typically work hard to build a heartfelt connection, and they are deeply committed to their partner.

Threes are highly adaptable, which means they can shape-shift their personality to be the best possible fit for what they believe is expected. In romantic relationships, there is an opportunity to see beneath this outer performance. Tenderness, attentive care, and deep loyalty often lie beneath a Three's impressive exterior. Threes are quite thoughtful and intentional in their romantic partnerships, and they appreciate when their partner is supportive and encouraging to them.

Levels of Development

When very unhealthy, Threes avoid failure at all costs. This concept is often applied to their work endeavors but can actually be true of relationships as well. If a Three perceives that they have failed in past relationships, they may be reluctant to enter a new one. They would rather avoid the shame and embarrassment of a relationship breaking down by cutting themselves off from others. In this state, a Three who is already in a relationship may stay in something that is unhealthy to avoid being seen as a failure, or they may constantly name, blame, and shame others to avoid being seen as insufficient by their partner. Unhealthy Threes can also be competitive with their partner.

In average levels of health, Threes can be self-promotional and highly image-conscious. They may share their achievements with their partner solely for recognition. Threes in this state may also be people pleasers who have lived their lives trying to meet what they believe others expect of them. They want their partner to be happy with them, too, so they might adapt who they are to be who their partner desires. Average Threes tend to have trouble balancing commitments. Because they want to be as impressive as possible, Threes may seek to impress those outside the relationship while neglecting their partner. This behavior can cause deep division. Average Threes might see their partner as someone with great untapped potential and push them to achieve the goals they have for them. Average Threes commit to having the best relationship they can, even if it requires that they do some things that are uncomfortable or vulnerable for them, like opening up about their feelings.

Healthy Threes know and accept themselves as they are. They want to be a better version of themselves, not for the sake of "winning" but for their own mental health and self-development. Healthy Threes deeply value relationships, and while they still seek to get tasks done, they don't let work or other practical needs overrun their real need for human connection. Healthy Threes value the humanity in themselves and their partner; rather than seeing people as projects, healthy Threes value humans simply for being.

Communication & Conflict

Threes want deep, emotionally fulfilling relationships, but sharing can be hard for them. Vulnerability can feel like an opportunity to let people see failure, and that feels too hard. It's important for Threes to have space with their partner to share and talk about life without feeling pressure to open up. If their partner goes first, a Three can often be more emotionally vulnerable.

One of the most challenging triggers for Threes is unfounded criticism. Like Ones, Threes work hard to be the best they can be. Average to healthy Threes feel comfortable to acknowledge and admit wrongdoing because they know deep down that feedback is the key to improvement. However, if a Three feels unjustly criticized, they may get defensive or frustrated. For the most part, Threes prefer direct, kind, and clear communication, which makes it easier for them to take relational feedback.

Part of the Three's desire for success is having a healthy relationship with their partner, so hearing that they've let their partner down can be severely disappointing. It's important to reassure Threes that they are loved and valued for who they are, even when conflict arises.

In conflict, Threes really try to figure things out. They may get frustrated or have an emotional response, but many Threes do their best to remain calm and rational because they believe competence and critical thinking will be the solution to the problem. This can cause other types to feel like the Three's approach is sterile, and Threes can come off as emotionally inhibited.

The emotion Threes exhibit most often is frustration, while their true feelings lie underneath. It's helpful to talk things out with Threes so they can have space to discuss how they truly feel. Effective communication is incredibly important for Threes in relationships, but it can sometimes take time to cultivate safe space to communicate well.

Enneagram study calls Threes to slow down, take a breath, observe themselves and their feelings, and better articulate their emotions in the moment.

Intimacy

Like most types, Threes need various types of intimacy to feel connected and fulfilled. Threes are in the Heart center, but they are often working so hard on their goals that they don't take time to feel, connect, or pause. Underneath their high-achieving exterior, Threes crave emotional connection, but they aren't always sure how to get it. Threes feel more connected when they feel valued and prioritized, and it's sometimes hard for them to open up, so they value and enjoy spending intentional time alone with their partner.

Vulnerability can be difficult for Threes. While some feel that physical intimacy is more vulnerable, and others emotional intimacy, most Threes need emotional intimacy to pave the way for sexual intimacy. In my research, Threes shared that having sex actually helped them to be more emotionally present in their relationship. Threes shared that sexual experiences help them feel grounded in the present, allowing them to be emotionally connected with their partner. While Threes seem highly self-assured, they need validation from their partner, especially when it comes to sex. Threes long to feel desired by their partner, and being verbally told how loved they are is helpful.

Average Threes generally feel the need to shape-shift to be who they believe is best in any relationship. As they grow more comfortable with a romantic partner, Threes let down their guard and no longer feel the need to act like a chameleon. Full comfort often means allowing their partner to see them when they aren't "on"—with no makeup, no pretenses, simply existing. Success in a romantic partnership isn't all about achievement for Threes; it's more focused on whether their partner is pleased with them. If their partner is happy—and they show it—a Three will feel secure and content. If not, a Three may work hard to be genuinely better for the relationship.

Key Points

FOR THREES

If you're a Three, you know you are committed to your partner, but it may be necessary to remind them how much you care. Your tunnel vision surrounding your goals and your constant forward motion can sometimes cause your partner to feel unimportant. Take time to focus on them without distraction. Your pace of life can leave you feeling exhausted, and as you learn to rest, you'll be more present and in touch with who you truly are and how you really feel. When you feel frustrated with yourself, your partner, or life in general, pause and consider what feelings lie beneath that surface emotion.

Threes aren't always able to show emotions in real time, but they do have them. Asking a Three to share their experience when they are given time to process can be eye-opening and good for the relationship. When Threes don't feel safe enough to be vulnerable, they won't share. Plan intentional quality time with a Three, and be patient if they can't explain exactly how they feel. Threes seem self-assured and confident, so you may not expect that they need encouragement from you, but they do. Offer encouragement, validation, and support, and your relationship will thrive.

FOUR: THE INDIVIDUALIST

Fours love deep emotional connection in relationships. They long to be seen and loved for who they are, and they spend a great deal of time considering their life, dreams, and identity. They are highly introspective, appreciate depth and intimacy, and express their positive and negative emotions. Fours are searching for their true soulmate.

Fours tend to get emotionally attached quickly. They sometimes forget that not everyone's emotional readiness matches theirs, and they can quickly get caught up in seeing the relationship as more than it is. This tendency can cause frustration at times, but it can also act as an invitation to others; a Four's investment in the relationship creates space for the partner to return the same level of dedication. Fours are highly affectionate, and they want their partner to feel seen, known, and valued.

Levels of Development

Unhealthy Fours can get lost in daydreams and believing that everyone else has something that they don't. They blame their partner for their unhappiness and become angry about their life and challenges. Their anger is often directed inward, but their general unhappiness can cause tension in the relationship, as

Fours can take the little things their partner does or doesn't do personally. When they get lost in their minds, Fours can detach from reality and lack awareness of the impact of their actions, words, and feelings on others. Unhealthy to average Fours fear abandonment. They tend to pull others in close with love, affection, and emotional connection, then push them away when they fear they could be hurt by letting someone in.

Fours in average levels of health ruminate on their feelings and emotional life, which is part of the reason they feel so strongly about their relationships. Average Fours are committed to fully feeling and expressing their emotions, so they sometimes withdraw to have more space and time to process. They are able to recognize that their partner cannot complete them, and cannot be the sole sounding board for their emotional experiences. Average Fours want to cultivate a deep understanding with their partner, so they will go to great lengths to deepen and expand the relationship. They long for a sense of being known and mirrored by their partner; if they don't feel that their partner understands how they feel, they may feel deeply unloved.

Healthy Fours are in tune with who they believe they are, and they are vulnerable in their successes and shortcomings. They bring a sense of true authenticity, beauty, and meaning to their relationships. They are highly intuitive and compassionate, and have the ability to sit with others and mirror their emotions. Healthy Fours support their partner's awareness of emotions, and help them see the value and necessity of giving proper space to process them. They cultivate deep emotional intimacy, and they are expressive of themselves and their love for their partner.

Communication & Conflict

Fours want to feel truly heard. It's more important that Fours feel heard than fixed when they talk about their feelings. When others try to fix what they are going through, Fours often feel that their experience is diminished, and they can feel incredibly misunderstood.

Their feelings are real, and it's important to listen and understand without judgment, critique, or pressure. Fours live inside their heads so much that sometimes people assume that there is something wrong if they aren't talking. This may be true, but Fours often just need time to process. Fours are deep feelers and thinkers, so allowing them to process when they need to will help build a good relationship.

Fours tend to express their authentic feelings as a way to get through disagreements. This can sometimes mean being openly emotional and confrontational, while other times it means withdrawing to think, and returning to the problem later. Either way, most Fours prefer to clear the air before they go about their day because they are so in tune with the emotional atmosphere. They are honest and present, and want others to be the same way.

Intimacy

Connection is very important for Fours. Long conversations, verbal expressions of love, complete openness, and physical closeness all build the intimacy Fours desire. Fours need to truly feel this emotional connection in order to open up to their partner. Fours enjoy discussing their hopes and dreams for the future, their buried thoughts and feelings, their past, their relationships, and more. Fours tend to invest themselves fully in their interests, so they always have much to talk about.

Fours feel both positive and negative emotions strongly, like an electric current. Their emotions can be all-encompassing at times, and emotional intimacy and attachment is based on how comfortable they feel sharing deep feelings with others. Fours sometimes build emotional intimacy by sharing vulnerability first. If this attempt at connection is dismissed or unreciprocated, Fours can feel hurt and isolated. They need to feel safe to continue to share.

Emotional intimacy and a safe, open, vulnerable relationship is more important than physical intimacy for the typically expressive, passionate Four. Sex is also deeply emotional for them, so if their partner and the relationship provide genuine care, authenticity, and connection, sex will be enjoyable and fulfilling. If Fours frequently feel diminished, misunderstood, or rejected by their partner, physical intimacy will be challenging.

The right combination of emotional and physical intimacy has an electric result. Fours tend to get emotionally attached fairly quickly, and sex that includes emotional intimacy amplifies that attachment. Fours want to be intimately connected with their partner in every sense.

Key Points

FOR FOURS

If you're a Four, you probably long for deep connection within yourself and with others. Your depth brings beauty and meaning in the world. One of the most remarkable aspects of your personality is the ability to show up fully in each moment. It is an act of courage to be as present as you often are, and your wide range of experience has made you strong. Know that even when your partner truly loves you, they may not be able to complete you in the way you hope. Allow your partner to begin to surprise you in new and meaningful ways.

FOR THOSE IN A RELATIONSHIP WITH A FOUR

If you are in a relationship with a Four, it's important to take them seriously. Fours can be witty and fun, yet they can feel misunderstood if teased for being sensitive, especially when they are expressing emotions. Their sensitivity is their strength. Love your Four by showing up for them, being present, and letting them know you care with intentional listening and empathy. Fours often express how they feel about others, and they appreciate when others offer the same. Grand gestures, thoughtful planning, and intimate conversation can all help your Four feel loved.

FIVE: THE OBSERVER

Fives are deeply loyal and committed in relationships. It often takes Fives quite some time to think through what they want and how to go about it, but they are kind and devoted once they are in a partnership. Fives enjoy thoughtful conversation, so they feel connected when they share ideas with their partner. Fives generally highly value solitude, yet quality time with their significant other is just as important for their well-being.

The outside world can overwhelm Fives, so they often need space in relationships to withdraw and isolate for a while. It's important that Fives feel free to take space when they need it. If they don't feel that they can do so, they will feel pressured and unable to show up as their best selves. Fives often appreciate partners who draw them out and help them experience the world outside their heads, and they feel most connected when they have long conversations with their partner. They don't let many people in, and once they do, they are loyal. Fives protect their own energy, so they tend to have a strong sense of personal boundaries. This goes both ways; they want others to respect their boundaries, and they won't intrude upon others in return.

Levels of Development

Unhealthy Fives retreat into the safety of their own minds, as interactions with others feel intrusive and unsafe. They become withdrawn and isolated and don't trust anyone else to be capable or competent. When very unhealthy, Fives don't even trust their own thoughts or ability to think rationally. Unhealthy Fives feel that they are no longer in control of their own energy reserves, so they become reclusive and antisocial. They often become cynical about the world and relationships. They will take any sense of genuine care or concern from a loved one as an intrusion, and this will result in further isolation. Unhealthy Fives hide from reality by withdrawing, isolating, and believing that their internal world is the only one they need.

Average Fives are steady and rational. They care deeply, but they are also guarded, especially with anyone outside their partnership. Fives invest themselves in a deep connection and a lasting partnership, but they can also become overwhelmed when they feel demands are placed on them by the outside world. They are comfortable with a partner who is independent and doesn't need them, but sometimes what Fives need is someone who can draw them out of their heads and into reality. Average Fives sometimes expect their partner to understand their silences, but it can be difficult for a partner to determine if a Five is angry, anxious, sad, or simply lost in thought. While Fives prioritize their independence, they sometimes do need help. A sign of true intimacy is a Five asking for help from their partner, rather than turning to their own research to find the answer.

Healthy Fives are wise and knowledgeable. Their keen observation skills make them perceptive and intuitive, so they are often able to offer a wise thought or pinpoint a helpful idea long before anyone else can. Healthy Fives are open to experiencing a range of connection, and they can balance their need to recharge in solitude with communicating their care for others. They are curious, and they learn and observe their partner so that they can love them in the best way possible. Healthy Fives find that the connection they are looking for comes from their romantic relationship, not just their connection with themselves. They see life as a series of giving and taking, so they are more open to giving of themselves and receiving love from others. Healthy Fives are not threatened by emotions, so they live a more fulfilled life, with mentally and emotionally close relationships.

Communication & Conflict

Fives have a lot to say, but sometimes they get a reputation for being quiet or aloof. They consider their thoughts and ideas carefully before they share, and if they feel these will be judged or dismissed, they may decide not to share at all. Fives generally don't say everything they think. They are intentional about what they say and may not be ready to respond to direct questions if they haven't thought through every aspect of a response. Fives tend to speak in complete thoughts or ideas, so when they are ready to share, it's helpful if others listen without interrupting until they have finished speaking.

Fives don't always vocalize their feelings. Instead, they prefer to separate themselves from their emotional life so that their thoughts aren't muddied by feelings. Fives are good at observing the world around them and are often attentive listeners. Fives are empathetic and deeply caring people, but just as they don't always share their own feelings, they sometimes don't express their empathy toward their partner.

Fives prefer to take space to think before engaging in conflict. They might get quiet or isolate themselves to find the space to think things through. Fives look for clarity and logic to sort through conflict, and they prefer not to let emotions get the best of them. Fives seek a sense of steadiness in their thoughts, but this detachment from emotion can sometimes lead to detachment from reality.

Partners of Fives might find it difficult to have healthy conflict because so much of it actually happens inside for Fives. Other types might process out loud or actively argue, but Fives often withdraw to a quiet place to think before they reengage. If forced to stay present through the conflict, Fives may shut down because they haven't had adequate time to gather their thoughts. Emotionally charged situations can be overwhelming for Fives, who often prefer to observe or analyze their feelings rather than feeling them. When they are able to deal with conflict, Fives seek clarity by focusing on the facts at hand and expressing them thoughtfully and calmly. Fives tend to be considerate of others, so their method of working through conflict feels like the most caring way they can approach it. Their approach can feel inconsiderate, however, when their partner doesn't understand it.

Intimacy

Like most types, Fives desire emotional connection and intimacy, yet they find stimulating conversation and mental connection just as important. When Fives feel emotionally and mentally connected with their partner, they can find the right headspace to be sexually intimate.

Fives have a hard time getting out of their heads and into their bodies. Many Fives feel like they can't turn off their mind, so mental connection is often a prerequisite for emotional connection. Trust and safety are incredibly important for Fives, so they don't often give of themselves freely right away. It takes them a while to open up, but they are capable of deep connection once they get there. In my research, some Fives expressed that they need sexual intimacy in order to get out of their heads.

Many Fives find that they need to reserve some emotional energy throughout the day to have enough left to engage in physical intimacy. Because Fives tend to isolate and withdraw when overwhelmed, feeling like they are depleted can prevent sexual intimacy with their partner. It's important to find a balance between planning ahead so the Five can save some energy and learning to be a bit more spontaneous.

Many Fives reported that they love being physically intimate with their partner, and it makes them feel safe and whole in the relationship. However, many Fives stated that it's too difficult to get out of their own heads, and they prefer not to be touched. In either case, it's important for a couple to discuss their individual responses to physical intimacy so they can love each other better.

Key Points

FOR FIVES

If you're a Five, you may tend to isolate yourself when you are feeling overwhelmed. Consider that being with people and engaging in thought-provoking conversation might energize you. Your deep commitment to your partner is likely important to you, but you may not talk about it often. Be sure to let your partner know how much you care about them with words and action. Build connection with your partner by inviting them into a hobby you enjoy. It might sound too intimate at first, but it can build a sense of connection that will sustain the relationship.

FOR THOSE IN A RELATIONSHIP WITH A FIVE

If you're in a relationship with a Five, you're probably familiar with their regular need to back away and find solitude. It's important to try not to take this personally. Fives need alone time to recharge, but that doesn't mean they don't love you deeply. It is important to avoid pressuring a Five as this can cause them to feel overwhelmed, and they may retreat further. Be sure to give them space, and if you do want to pull them in, invite—rather than demand—them to connect. Many Fives have always felt like misfits in the world, so it can be validating to feel that you want to hear what they think and feel. Ask your partner what they are interested in and learn from their expertise. Even if you aren't particularly interested in the topic, a Five will feel loved if they feel that you are genuinely interested in their thoughts.

SIX: THE LOYALIST

Sixes are committed and loyal in relationships. They seek a trustworthy and consistent partner who helps quiet their constant self-questioning. Sixes are often suspicious of others at first and may be highly skeptical of a potential partner's motives. Once they have built a foundation of trust, Sixes are in it for the long haul. They are fun, witty, and kind, and they deeply value good relationships. Sixes often find a partner who is calm where they are anxious, and bold where they are fearful.

Sixes are also highly responsible, so they often take on all the tasks in a relationship—from planning the calendar to cleaning the kitchen—to make sure they get done. Planning can help them calm their fears. Sixes make great friends, and the basis of a romantic relationship with a Six is often deep, faithful friendship. Sixes tend to be cautious, so feeling emotionally safe is important to them. They tend to analyze and overthink interactions, looking for any sign that they may not be safe or accepted. At times, they second-guess the relationship. It's important that partners reassure them if they express doubt, rather than taking offense that the Six would question them.

Levels of Development

When unhealthy, Sixes are highly suspicious and fearful of others. A Six might become so fearful that their partner is going to leave that they drive a wedge between them, ending the relationship. Unhealthy Sixes may test their partner's loyalty, and if they don't pass, Sixes take it as further evidence that no one is trustworthy. Sixes in this state tend to overanalyze every interaction, finding all the little ways their partner might hint that they are going to abandon them. Sixes tend to push people away and pull them in simultaneously because they fear abandonment and want what is comfortable. As a result, unhealthy Sixes may find themselves continually returning to a toxic relationship, simply because it is what they know.

When at an average level of health, Sixes are both suspicious and incredibly committed. They may fear that their partner will leave, but they are also committed to growing together. These mixed signals can lead to some confusion, but reassurance and physical touch can help them through it. Sixes can feel comforted and steadied by depth and trust, so they appreciate openness and vulnerability from their partner that makes them feel more connected. Average Sixes are witty, engaging, and loyal in their relationships. They need reassurance that everything is okay, and they feel most secure when their partner maintains close contact.

Healthy Sixes are loving, trusting, and affectionate. They commit themselves to people and causes, and they are more decisive about what they want and how they would like to move forward. Healthy Sixes are devoted to their loved ones, and make excellent romantic partners because they are secure, stable, and predictable, yet fun. Sixes can be very witty, and they feel connected to their partner when they enjoy humor and laughter together. Sixes generally see the worst that can happen, but healthy Sixes also focus on the best. They need less reassurance to know that everything will be okay because they don't get caught up in questioning or overanalyzing.

Communication & Conflict

Like Ones, Sixes prioritize honesty over almost anything else, and no truth could be worse than a lie. If something bad happens, they would like to hear about it in a clear, concise, and honest way. When they seem fearful, it's because they have already thought about the negative things that could happen; when something bad comes up, it doesn't necessarily surprise them, so they are equipped to handle it.

Sixes often share their fears and worries with their partner. When their partner expresses frustration with their anxiety or attempts to refute their worries, this can make things much worse. It's most helpful to validate their worries, while also giving them space to process the ideas they are concerned about. When a Six feels they have space to process in this way, they feel the safety they are searching for, and often find that their concerns may not be realistic.

Sixes are often defensive and reactive in conflict. Conflict threatens their sense of security, and they will do almost anything to avoid this. Some Sixes can feel flustered in conflict and may need some space to think through things, while others are ready and willing to engage in argument.

At times, Sixes avoid conflict because it makes them feel unsafe, but typically their desire to make sure everything is okay wins out, and they will confront their fear to save the relationship. As with many types, communication is a priority for Sixes. Not only do they need to feel like everything is okay, but they also want to understand their own feelings, and why the conflict happened in the first place. As they process with their partner, they can find reassurance, connection, and steps to avoid future confrontation.

Intimacy

Sixes need quality time together to feel safe and loved, and they want to create a sense of "home" with their partner. Quality time, complete honesty, and open communication help a Six feel comfortable and safe in the relationship; that safety is a prerequisite for both emotional and physical intimacy. Sixes tend to build emotional connection on a foundation of friendship. Fully knowing a Six requires patience, as they tend to be cautious about who they let in, but once they feel mutual trust they desire complete vulnerability.

When Sixes feel safe, they are thoroughly invested in their relationships, yet sometimes they fear that their partner doesn't share the same depth of commitment. A reassuring word or thoughtful gesture helps remind a Six that their partner is present and cares deeply about them. Intention and thoughtfulness are the best ways to build emotional intimacy with a Six. They can sense when others aren't genuine, so faking it can erode their trust. When healthy and engaged, Sixes are thoughtful, thorough, and attentive, and they offer their partner the same stability and kindness that they seek.

Sixes also often need to feel safety and connection before they can be physically intimate. Mutual trust, patience, and relational health are important prerequisites for sex, and they need to know that this intimate part of their lives won't be shared outside their partnership. When surveyed, many Sixes shared that they sometimes need reassurance or affirmation that they are doing well in the bedroom, as they tend to question themselves. A kind, affirming word can help build trust and connection here.

Sixes are thinking types who can get wrapped up in thought and have a hard time being present in the moment. Being in the right emotional place can help, but more important, Sixes need to build intimacy over time. Intentional, caring touches throughout the day—such as a back rub or holding hands—can help build the foundation for a Six to be sexually intimate later. Physical engagement can actually help calm a Six's tendency to overthink. Sixes are often passionate people, so the connection can be powerful when cultivated with intention and care.

Key Points

FOR SIXES

Your depth of commitment to your partner creates great stability for both of you. Some Sixes need constant reassurance, causing you to lack trust in your partner and the relationship. Try identifying ways your partner has shown their commitment. Frequent questioning can sometimes lead to insecurity; try to focus on the good in your partner and relationship rather than what could go wrong. Some Sixes, however, find that their romantic relationship is the only thing in their lives that they don't question. It is healing to find security and trust in a relationship with another human, and with yourself.

FOR THOSE IN A RELATIONSHIP WITH A SIX

It's important to listen when a Six opens up and shares their anxieties and fears. Sixes feel deeply misunderstood and rejected when others show frustration with their anxious thoughts. Try asking them questions about it and giving them space to process rather than diminishing their fear. Asking "What would we do if that happened?" can calm their fears better than "That will never happen." If you're in a relationship with a Six, always be truthful with them, as even white lies can undermine their trust. Show a Six you care by planning a thoughtful date, making time to intentionally connect with them, and reassuring them when they feel unsteady.

SEVEN: THE ENTHUSIAST

Sevens are fun-loving, exuberant, and often expressive and whimsical people who bring light and joy everywhere they go. Because of their lighthearted nature, others sometimes think Sevens are too flighty to commit to a relationship, but this isn't necessarily true. When they find the right partner for them, Sevens are deeply loyal. If they feel that their partner won't run from the relationship, Sevens are less likely to flee.

Sevens tend to be fairly independent, yet they also truly want to make their partner happy. Sevens love a partner who helps them feel both free and grounded. Sevens in a long-term partnership find ways to get the most out of life with their partner. Sevens sometimes grow tired of feeling like they have to be the fun one in every relationship, so they will be able to go deeper if a partner is able to release that expectation and let them be the fullest version of themselves.

Levels of Development

When unhealthy, Sevens feel stifled by the care and nurturing of others. They tend to have an addictive personality and are always looking for more from life—more fun, drink, food, sex, adrenaline. Impulsive, anxious, and fiercely independent, they may run from emotional connection because they believe that a relationship can only result in pain and misery. Unhealthy Sevens prefer to be physically or mentally alone, because that is the only way to avoid being trapped. They can become strict, rigid, and perfectionist—the opposite of their normal personality pattern.

Sevens in average levels of health are fun and bright. They might feel occasionally stifled by relationships, but they also commit to their loved ones. Average Sevens avoid feeling too sentimental because they aren't sure what the future will hold. They run headlong into the next opportunity. Sevens in this state may find their partners to be either an exciting challenge or deadweight on their journey. Average Sevens say yes more than they say no, and they always have a fun new adventure on the horizon, with or without their partner. Once average Sevens are committed to a relationship, they try to make their partner feel loved, happy, and satisfied. They are upfront about who they are, and look for the same authenticity in others. Sevens often struggle to be vulnerable, so it takes time for them to open up emotionally and fully commit.

Healthy Sevens radiate light and exuberance, tempered with a good dose of reality. Healthy Sevens can find the beauty, joy, and meaning in the good as well as the bad. They aren't afraid to see the challenging parts of life, and they are present and connected in the moment. Their enthusiasm doesn't drive them into the future, but keeps them grounded in the present.

They are intimately connected with their partner, and give themselves to the relationship. Rather than chasing their own pursuits, they look for opportunities to chase together. Less healthy Sevens tend to reject their own feelings, but healthy Sevens are able to hold the positive and negative halves of the emotional spectrum in balance.

Communication & Conflict

Sevens are positive and upbeat communicators. They don't like to get bogged down by negativity, and appreciate others who keep an open mind. Sevens can sometimes seem argumentative because they often say the first thing that comes to their mind. Perhaps some Sevens enjoy a good debate, but they are often just throwing ideas out there. Conversations are an opportunity for them to brainstorm. They want to be taken seriously, but they don't need to work out the logistics of their ideas in the present moment; the practicalities can come later.

Sevens don't often offer up their own feelings. Their joyful demeanor can cause others to assume that they are never hurt by stinging comments, but that's mostly because they don't show it. Sevens do have feelings, but they don't often communicate or think about them. Negative emotions are particularly difficult for Sevens to think about, even though they know they are normal in a healthy romantic relationship. Offering Sevens time to process before they share can help.

Sevens generally have a hard time with conflict because it requires wading into the negativity that they work so hard to avoid. If they realize conflict is inevitable, Sevens like to stay on the bright side, and clear it up as quickly as possible so that they can return to their happy and peaceful existence. This can sometimes cause others to feel like Sevens aren't present, so it's helpful for them to remember that the real happiness they want requires properly dealing with conflict first.

Sevens tend to make jokes to ease tense situations. Less healthy Sevens tend to have a difficult time owning that their words or actions hurt someone else. It helps to frame situations in "I" language to communicate better with a Seven: "When you said this, I felt that." This language can take some of the pressure off, and offer a better foundation for conflict. Deep down, Sevens avoid this type of confrontation because they don't want to admit that what they did hurt their partner. This is motivated by their desire to make their partner happy and satisfied; hearing that their partner is upset can make them feel like they failed to do what their partner needed.

Intimacy

Sevens don't readily trust everyone with their emotional needs, so sharing them cultivates real emotional intimacy. Sevens tend to have many interests, and feel connected to their partner when they are able to talk about all their hobbies with them. They also feel deeply connected when they don't have to be the fun one; if they can relax and let their guard down, there is a unique sense of love that both parties can enjoy.

Sevens often like spontaneity, fun, and trying new things. In my research, I found that while Sevens enjoy sex, sometimes their minds are rushing to the next thing and they are flippant about it in the moment. Emotional connection cultivated over time helps Sevens be more present in the moment. Many Sevens enjoy active sex lives and want the most out of their time with their partner. Sevens deeply want to make their partner happy, and physical intimacy is one avenue for that.

When asked, most Enneagram types shared that emotional intimacy must come before physical intimacy, but Sevens shared that sometimes having sex is easier than creating emotional connection. That doesn't mean that sex fills their need for intimacy; in fact, many Sevens mentioned that they feel more fulfilled when physical and emotional intimacy go hand in hand.

Sevens can seem openhearted and whimsical, and many are very sensitive to others, yet they are still thinking types. This means that they use their minds to take in and process information more than they use their physical or emotional faculties. Creating space for emotional intimacy often requires intentional time and connecting while doing something else. Most of all, it's important to know that Sevens may take time to emotionally commit, but once they do, they are deep, loyal, and can be more emotionally expressive.

Key Points

Tapping into vulnerability can be difficult, especially at first, but because you value authenticity, it's worth prioritizing. You seek fulfillment and satisfaction in life, yet the true satisfaction you long for may lie in relationships, not in increased independence. How has avoiding emotion affected your relationship? In what small way can you show up fully today? As a Seven, you're known for being full of courage. Today, consider how vulnerability can be powerful, and can help you find the joy you are looking for.

FOR THOSE IN A RELATIONSHIP WITH A SEVEN

If you are in a relationship with a Seven, it's important that they feel that you want to be present with them in the fun things. Sevens often feel like others are trying to get them to live in the present, but the present doesn't offer anything interesting or engaging. Show that you care by being engaged and authentic with them in the moment. Show a Seven they are loved by surprising them with a fun activity, and make sure to appreciate their humor and exuberance along the way.

EIGHT: THE CHALLENGER

In relationships, Eights are passionate, purposeful, and invested. On their own, Eights work hard to protect themselves from control and betrayal by building a tough exterior, but in a committed partnership, they let their walls down and allow their partner to see the deep kindness and tenderness they carry for their loved ones.

Eights tend to protect their partner and the relationship, and they do their best to prevent intrusions between themselves and their partner. Eights show up fully in their relationships, and desire a genuine, authentic connection. While typically not very emotional, Eights are intuitive, so they can tell who is trustworthy and who is disingenuous. Eights are loyal, and trust is very important to them. If they find their partner is dishonest, they will lose trust, and it will be difficult to rebuild. For this reason, Eights take time to open up; they need a solid foundation before they are comfortable enough to trust and be vulnerable. They are forthright and honest, and they appreciate when a partner has the courage to disagree with them. They want a partnership, which intuitively means give-and-take.

Levels of Development

Unhealthy Eights can be aggressive and brash. They show little regard for the feelings of others, and seem to suck the air out of any room they enter. Unhealthy Eights can badger others into doing what they want, and feel the need to control everyone and everything around them. They can be possessive of their partner, or believe their partner wants to control them. They resist vulnerability to avoid betrayal.

Average Eights are assertive and tend to pursue what they want in life. They are usually decisive and in tune with their desires and will act on their own beliefs and needs. For average Eights, the underlying motivation for most of their actions is resisting control. At times, they may brush off their partner's feelings or ideas when making decisions because they believe they know what is right. They can be tender, but if they don't share a deep level of trust with their partner, they may be a bit defensive. Average Eights want a deep, meaningful connection, and desire emotional intimacy even if they aren't always certain how to create it. They are hardworking and often dedicate themselves to cultivating a life that supports their partner's material needs.

Healthy Eights are loving, gracious, and generous. They are confident and decisive, yet they understand when their decisions affect others. They often choose what is best for all parties, not just themselves. They see potential in their partner, and work to bring out the best in them. They are loyal, trustworthy, and devoted. They allow their partner to see their vulnerability, and find this tenderness a strength rather than a weakness. Healthy Eights have learned to pause before they react, and this helps them cultivate stronger relationships.

Communication & Conflict

Eights are passionate in everything they do. They speak, act, fight, and love with great intensity. This intensity is often mis-understood as anger or negative emotion, which can be really challenging for Eights who simply want the truth to be spoken. Eights often come off stronger than they intend, and it's hard when those around them assume the worst of their passionate communication style.

Eights speak declaratively; one of their tactics to avoid being controlled is to assert their thoughts with such authority that they can't be disputed. Eights actually might want to open a conversation, but because their style of speaking is often more self-assured, their partner can think that the Eight is trying to have the final word. It's important to note that an Eight's anger isn't necessarily directed at their partner and is more often aimed at the injustice and dishonesty they see around them. Sometimes they even sound angry when they aren't angry at all! Passionate Eights give themselves fully to their ideas and opinions, sometimes loudly.

Eights tend to confront conflict head-on. They don't often beat around the bush and believe that the best and fastest way to resolve something is for everyone to speak their mind, unfiltered. Eights aren't typically conflict avoidant, but average to healthy Eights aren't looking for a fight. Connection sometimes comes from a heated debate, but Eights more often find emotional intimacy from the feeling of being deeply known and loved.

The Enneagram is particularly helpful with Eights, who often hear their whole lives that they are too much or too overwhelming for people around them. Eights have needed their strength and passion to get through life. They can be warm and inviting, but that's not their primary temperament. Learning the Enneagram can help Eights and their partners understand that the anger many Eights express isn't meant to be personal. Eights are typically all-or-nothing types, either all-in or all-out, who tend to speak with full force at full volume. Others can feel intimidated by the Eight's presence, even though that wasn't their intended effect. Eights truly want deep connection, but they are so used to feeling judged for the way they communicate that they will move on if they feel misunderstood.

Intimacy

Eights tend to be guarded until they feel really safe, so sometimes it's easier for them to engage in physical intimacy than emotional intimacy. It takes time for Eights to build the trust they need to be truly vulnerable and feel connected with their partner. Eights have a tough exterior, so others sometimes assume that they don't have or care about feelings. Eights, however, simply don't express many emotions other than anger when they are not comfortable. Building the trust and comfort necessary for Eights to fully show up in a relationship takes time.

Eights must feel like their partner is attentive to them, especially when they are vulnerable, in order to find the emotional intimacy they need. It's important for Eights to feel heard and valued, rather than dismissed, when they share intimate feelings. The best thing you can offer an Eight to build vulnerability is undistracted time. Sometimes this means doing something enjoyable together, such as hiking or exploring a new restaurant, and other times it means simply being in the same room. Either way, connection is built through feeling heard and understood. If an Eight feels that their partner isn't invested or doesn't take them seriously, they won't waste their time on the relationship.

Communication is important for Eights, since they often feel misunderstood. It is important that physical intimacy feels reciprocal. Eights sometimes feel that physical intimacy is easier to cultivate than emotional, but that doesn't necessarily mean they don't also want the emotional side. In fact, sometimes the physicality leads to greater emotional connection.

Initiating can feel vulnerable for Eights if they are not sure they will be accepted. Eights can be risk takers in general, but they often look for a sure thing in love. If they feel there is a give-and-take in who initiates, they are more likely to feel loved and wanted by their partner, leading to a stronger relationship in the long run.

Key Points

FOR EIGHTS

As an Eight, boundaries have kept you safe throughout your life. They have been important barriers to keep your heart from betrayal by others who didn't respect or value you. Consider that your boundaries have also at times isolated you from others. Can you see the strength in choosing to be vulnerable? Have you found value in allowing yourself to connect emotionally? Sometimes that emotional connection is made possible by focusing on the voice of others rather than feeling the need to have the last word. In your relationship, how can you reach out to your partner today to cultivate a stronger emotional connection?

FOR THOSE IN A RELATIONSHIP WITH AN EIGHT

Eights are among the most misunderstood Enneagram types. Eights often express their passion and even anger surrounding injustice or lack of protection in the world, but this doesn't mean they are mad at their partner. Try to give them space to feel how they feel, whether that means allowing them to express their anger without taking it personally, giving them permission to be vulnerable, or joining them in happiness or excitement. Eights often resist attempts by others to control their "inappropriate" emotions. Be a safe space for them by allowing them to be themselves.

NINE: THE PEACEMAKER

Nines offer a warm, comforting, gentle presence in relationships. They want to create a harmonious and loving dynamic, and they offer a sense of steadiness and support to their partner. Nines are sometimes called the "darlings" of the Enneagram (Cron & Stabile, 2016) because they can be so easy to get along with. They endear themselves to others with their peaceable nature and general positivity. Nines are fair, even-keeled, and able to understand and value various perspectives on the same issue.

Nines typically don't appreciate being pressured by others, and they especially dislike feeling that others expect them to perform or be a certain way. They tend to be accepting of others as a result and avoid placing expectations on their partner.

Levels of Development

When unhealthy, Nines withdraw and avoid anything that could rock their internal sense of peace. Because the world is full of challenges that could shake them off balance, unhealthy Nines shut everything and everyone out. They become complacent in their relationship and are ambivalent about their partner. They numb their feelings and experiences by doing something—eating, drinking, playing video games, watching

TV, reading, and sleeping—to keep their mind off of their deep sense of unease. Bouts of numbing might be punctuated by fits of anger.

Nines in average levels of health are more engaged in their relationship, but they may not have found their voice yet. Perhaps not believing that their thoughts and opinions matter, they go along with what their partner says to keep the peace. Nines sometimes convince themselves that they really agree even though they don't. At other times they say yes in the moment to avoid conflict, but later dig in their heels and passively refuse to cooperate without further discussion. Average Nines can be warm and thoughtful and want to make their relationship a place of comfort for themselves and for their partner. When they get comfortable, they may get complacent, and stop doing the little things that make their partner feel valued. If their partner can share how this makes them feel, it can help a Nine resume doing things that make their partner feel loved.

Healthy Nines have found their voice. They bring the same calming presence, along with true peace. They understand that a little conflict actually supports their goals of peace rather than detracts from them. They know that it's often worth it to stand up for themselves, and they've found a way to do so gracefully. Healthy Nines are stable, quietly self-assured, and able to look at things objectively. They offer their partner safety and comfort without feeling the need to conform entirely to their partner's personality. Healthy Nines lean into the relationship rather than zoning out when they feel pushed, and they are better able to verbalize their thoughts and feelings.

Communication & Conflict

Nines often need to take a step back to think things through when communicating. They sometimes nod to let others know they've heard them, but this doesn't mean they actually agree. Many Nines know what they want and need deep down, but they don't feel confident that others will listen if they speak. As a result, Nines often find themselves in situations where their partner has stopped expecting them to voice their opinion. It can be helpful to ask Nines specifically what they think or feel, but it's important that their partner feels like a safe person to tell. Nines often shut down if they feel interrupted or dismissed, so they need to feel heard in order to continue offering their ideas.

Nines in a committed relationship often become more vocal as they become more comfortable. Sometimes that can cause tension, but if a Nine is really passionate about something, they are okay with stirring things up a little. Nines tend to withdraw when pushed, and they can be very stubborn.

Because their motivation is so centered around getting along and having peace, Nines don't like conflict in general, and it can feel like a threat. Nines like to stay positive and avoid conflict if they can, but if they can't, communication is key! Nines prioritize talking through things fully until they reach peace again. As they grow, Nines find that a little conflict is a part of any healthy relationship, and a signal that two people are showing up for each other with their full ideas, thoughts, opinions, and emotions. Conflict doesn't seem so scary in that context.

The Enneagram can help Nines understand that they may not be in tune with their own needs and desires. Some Nines know exactly what they want and are comfortable with vocalizing it if they feel safe and heard. Many, however, have fallen asleep to who they really are, and find themselves merging with the strongest personality around them. Communication is crucial for Nines, and talking things out will help them learn more about themselves, who they are, and what they want in life.

Intimacy

Nines seek comfort and harmony, which they find in their relationships by spending quality time with their partner. It's important for Nines to feel emotionally connected, and they appreciate patience, gentleness, and kindness in conversation as a way to create emotional intimacy. Nines sometimes feel invisible in the world, so letting them know they are seen, heard, and loved is important in building an emotional connection. Nines tend to feel valued and connected when they engage in heartfelt conversation with their partner and when they do something fun!

Physical intimacy can be very emotional for many Nines, so they need to reserve some of their energy throughout the day to fully engage. They tend to be very passionate about those they love and are considerate in creating a deep and personal space together.

In my research, many Nines shared that they need to spend time with their partner taking care of each other and being emotionally connected before jumping into bed. Nines don't always initiate or ask for intimacy, but that doesn't mean they don't want it. It takes courage and energy for many Nines to be vulnerable enough to make the first move, so it helps when their partner acknowledges and appreciates the effort. Nines often need to feel fully comfortable before they decide to share what they really want or need, and they want to feel respected and cared for rather than pressured. For many Nines, being heard, valued, and loved are important stepping stones toward intimacy later; it's not necessarily easy to separate that emotional safety from the physical act of sex.

Nines can take a passive role in their public lives, but sometimes they enjoy being more assertive in private. Some Nines feel that who they are in the bedroom is the opposite of who they are in the rest of life, so rather than being passive, they prefer to take control. They enjoy making their partner happy, and they will be fully present when they feel emotionally engaged in intimacy.

Key Points

Showing up fully in relationships can be difficult, especially when it feels like the pressures of the world are never-ending. As a Nine, demands can be especially exhausting, even when you genuinely want to be present and connected with your partner. Become more integrated and action-oriented in your body by doing something physical, such as exercise or breathwork. These simple ways of engaging can help you be more present and create the connected relationship you want, while also reminding you that you have agency in your life. You will have true peace when you speak up for what you really want.

FOR THOSE IN A RELATIONSHIP WITH A NINE

If you are with a Nine and they choose to share something with you, stop what you're doing and listen. Nines often feel invisible in the world, so it's important that they feel acknowledged and seen by their partner. When Nines open up, they need a partner to show they are listening by avoiding interruption, nodding, and repeating what they say. These simple steps can help a Nine feel heard and understood. If a Nine says no, it has taken great courage to do so. If they are pushed, they tend to dig in their heels and become stubborn. Communication is key to work through these moments.

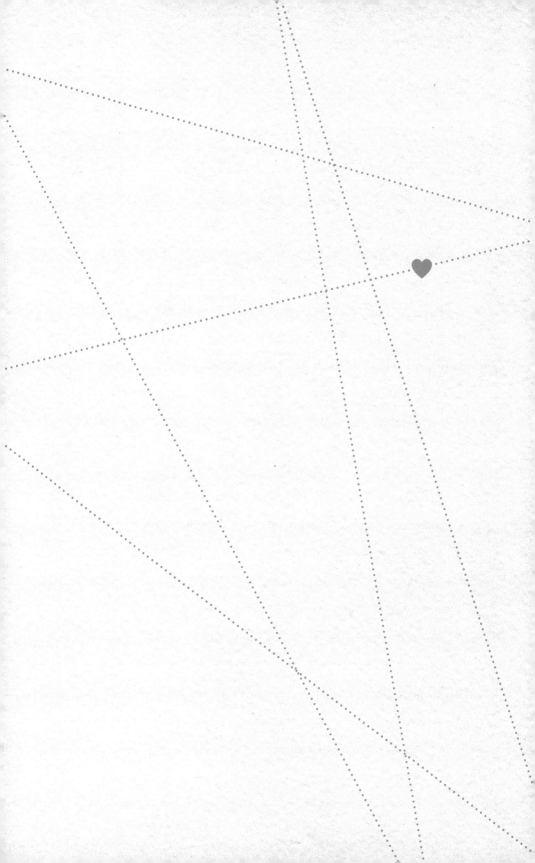

The Interplay

Each Enneagram type pairing has a specific alchemy. We often think that no other couples share our particular struggles in romantic relationships, yet as I've written on this topic, I've heard time and again that the Enneagram type pairing descriptions are uncannily accurate. On a personal note, when I first read about the interplay between my type and my husband's, I was blown away by not only how well it described our relationship but also how accurately it identified our areas of growth.

As you read, keep a few things in mind. First, note that same-type pairings are less common. While this book does not delve into the topic of subtypes, they are important to understand, especially if you and your partner share the same Enneagram type. (To learn more, I've included two books by subtype expert, Dr. Beatrice Chestnut [see page 186]). Wings and family of origin communication styles add important nuance when two people of the same type are in a relationship.

Second, if you were hoping to use the Enneagram as a roadmap to your next date, I've got bad news for you: there is no such thing as a "most compatible" Enneagram pairing. This insight often leaves love-seekers disappointed, but relationships are ultimately about people who are working toward growth and health as individuals, who are willing to show up and do the hard work in relationships, and who are kind, loving, and responsive to their partners. That's it. Any pairing can work well if you're willing to put in the effort. So here's the good news: if you are already in a relationship, you can breathe a sigh of relief knowing that you are not with the wrong Enneagram type.

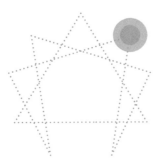

1-1

Two Ones might find themselves to be well-matched in a relationship. Ones tend to be conscientious, respectful, and responsible, and in most areas of life they are used to taking on all the responsibility. When partnered with another type One, a One may feel some release; their partner shares the load without being asked, and they don't have to do it all. Integrity is important in any relationship, but for Ones, it is perhaps the highest value. Integrity and honesty from both partners is an absolute requirement for trust, and Ones prioritize trust over nearly anything else.

Ones also value mutual respect. They are intentional and careful in their words and actions, and they are particular about personal character. Because they can understand what it feels like to have a strong inner critic, Ones might encourage each other to be more positive, gracious, and tolerant of their own faults. Alternatively, the presence of an inner critic on both ends could be a blind spot. It might be easy to forget that not everyone experiences life or self-talk in this unique way, and they may neglect to step outside it.

Ones like to have fun, but they typically set it aside until they complete everything else that needs to get done in a day. They often don't feel like they have completed enough tasks to indulge in a little leisure. When Ones are paired with other types, there can be more balance in this dynamic, but two Ones together need to make intentional space for fun and hold to it. A weekend getaway, a night out, or even an afternoon walk could help release some of the need to hold everything together and allow for deeper connection.

STRENGTHS: Ones support each other and help their partner feel like there is balance in the relationship.

AREAS TO WORK ON: Both tend to dig in their heels, and unaddressed anger can leak out as resentment, creating a chasm in the relationship. Work on releasing rigidity, and practice seeing different perspectives.

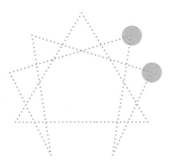

1 - 2

A One and a Two can make a great pair! Both tend to do what is necessary and pay attention to the people and tasks right in front of them. They are action-takers who sense what needs to be done, and they do it because their desire is to make the world a better place for those around them. The One has a harsh inner critic that is softened by the Two's patience and kindness. The Two tends to be warm and encouraging, with genuine love for their partner. The Two often feels like they are the only person helping or giving, but the One's consistency and responsibility can help the Two feel like they are in it together. The One is often attentive to the things their loved one cares most about, regardless of type, and they work hard to please their partner.

Together, a One and a Two value doing the right thing, doing what is best for others, and being a positive, kind presence in the world. Both can act as role models for those around them, and they often become pillars of their community. The One and the Two both feel responsible for the well-being of those around them to an extent, and this can be a good thing or a bad thing. Because they care about the welfare of others, they also care deeply about each other and are generous and intentional with their time and resources. On the other hand, they may overextend themselves at times, which can lead to exhaustion, burnout, and even resentment.

The Enneagram can highlight the specific ways self-care can help bring balance to each type. The One and the Two often need a little nudge to release some of the expectations of themselves and others, and to take time to care for themselves. Their constant work toward developing others can actually hinder the connection they both desire, if they neglect to focus on personal growth. Twos and Ones both need to remember to focus energy *inward* as well as *outward.*

STRENGTHS: Ones and Twos both value intentionality, conscientiousness, and integrity. They focus on fostering consideration for each other.

AREAS TO WORK ON: Both want to give of themselves to make the world a better place, but Ones tend to be more task-oriented and Twos more people-oriented. The One's desire to stick to logic over feelings can feel sterile and rigid to the Two, whose positivity and passion can feel too emotional for the One.

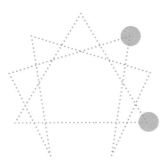

1-3

A One and a Three can be an impressive pairing of task-oriented, accomplished high achievers. The One admires the Three's can-do attitude and optimism, while the Three appreciates the One's attention to detail and thoughtfulness. The way they go about achieving even similar goals often differs. When things are going well, they will find each other supportive, competent, caring partners.

Ones and Threes are committed to being the best versions of themselves. Emotions can sometimes feel like obstacles, but both can learn to appreciate the effect that working through feelings has on their personal development. They tend to create rhythms and structures together that support their relationship. It's important to make space for fun and play in the calendar, so those routines don't feel like just another item on the to-do list.

The One and the Three each bring something valuable to the relationship. The Three's unshakable confidence in their partner's true potential can minimize the One's inner critic. With the Three in their corner, the One feels like they can do anything. The One's presence and consistency can ease the Three's tendency to live in the future. When things aren't going well, the One might find the Three's shape-shifting dishonest—remember, dishonesty is relational kryptonite for a One—and the Three might find the One's principled approach rigid and stifling.

STRENGTHS: Both Ones and Threes highly productive and appreciate that they can depend on each other.

AREAS TO WORK ON: Both tend to put feelings aside for the sake of getting things done. Ones are more likely to process their feelings later, while Threes tend to move on entirely. Learning how to truly feel and find space for rest is key.

1-4

Striking a balance seems to be the most important aspect of building a good connection in most Enneagram type pairings. This is definitely true for Fours and Ones together—both idealists with a vision of what the world could be. The Four can tend to be more whimsical, self-expressive, and openhearted—powerful traits that can help the One reconnect with their inner thoughts and feelings. The One tends to be a more rigid black-and-white thinker, so the Four's openness can help the One think more flexibly.

These types both seek depth and meaning in their relationships and look for excellence and beauty in life. Their aim is to observe and perfect an imperfect world. A One and Four couple may cultivate a beautiful home or curate an interesting book collection. The One can feel deeply seen and known by the Four, who can often see ways that the One needs to be affirmed and validated to silence their inner critic. In return, the One can see the Four's highest potential, and show them that they are capable of meeting it.

Both types tend to take feedback quite personally, which is a challenge. When the Four suggests that the One loosen up, and the One suggests that the Four get their act together, communication can deteriorate rapidly. It's especially important in this relationship to interact with genuine kindness, grace, and love, and to offer words of affirmation whenever possible.

STRENGTHS: Both Ones and Fours can be visionaries who seek excellence. While opposites, they can balance each other well.

AREAS TO WORK ON: A Four and a One can easily fall into mourning the ways the world is less than ideal. It's productive to notice and talk about the good around them as well; it will help this pair to grow in empathy toward one another. The Four can feel like the One is trying to fix them, while the One can feel like the Four is too expressive. Working to understand the other's perspective will improve their bond.

1-5

Ones and Fives can tend to have a lot in common. Both are thoughtful and apply themselves to everything they do. They spend time and energy getting to know each other well and appreciate the steadiness the other offers. The One likes the Five's depth, competence, and careful consideration, while the Five tends to feel supported by the One's high standards and attention to detail.

Both types tend to be independent and prefer to spend time alone to process and think, which helps this pair avoid feeling overwhelmed by each other. The relationship can be stable and dependable, especially since both the One and the Five prefer to remain rational and logical rather than allowing emotions to interfere with their communication.

The Five tends to be curious and interested in obscure topics. Their inquisitive nature keeps things interesting, especially if the One is willing to explore or learn about the topics as well. The One is more action-oriented in general, often concerned with taking care of all the practical things needed to help the relationship thrive. It might take a while to build the deep loyalty and trust they crave, but both types tend to be in it for the long haul once the foundation is set.

When the One makes a decision, their mind is not easily changed. They hold fast to their convictions and can argue their points perfectly. The Five, however, allows their ideas to evolve as they learn new information. As a result, the Five may grow frustrated that the One seems so rigid, while the One may feel that the Five is unpredictable.

STRENGTHS: In different ways, the One and the Five both bring a sense of calm and steadiness to the relationship.

AREAS TO WORK ON: Feedback may cause the One to feel as deficient as their inner critic constantly tells them they are. The One's advice can feel like criticism to the Five, causing the Five to need to withdraw to regain their energy. It's important for both types to offer gentleness, affirmation, and space when bringing things up.

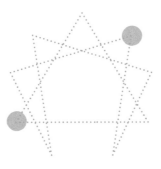

1-6

Ones and Sixes are both committed, courteous, and responsible. They value loyalty and duty in their relationship and community and are often thinking of little ways the world could be better, safer, and more livable for everyone. Like a One and Five relationship, a One-Six relationship tends to build slowly, but is secure and loyal once both partners feel safe. Deep trust is a requirement.

The Six can appreciate that the One brings structure and responsibility, and the Six will feel grounded and at ease through the One's confidence and attention to detail. The One appreciates that the Six offers wit, forethought, and deep friendship to the One's more serious demeanor. The One enjoys fun, but they often feel that they have to be responsible first. When together, a One and a Six share mutual responsibility, offering them both an opportunity to lighten up since neither partner is carrying all the weight.

Both the One and the Six like predictability. Fortunately for this pair, each is highly dependable and consistent. Life can feel chaotic for either type when things feel like they are constantly changing, so the routines and systems they implement will help calm the One's rigidity and the Six's anxiety. Their challenge is not to get too stuck in them.

Sixes often need connection to feel that a relationship is safe and steady, and they really appreciate when their partner checks in with them. When Ones become resentful or quiet, Sixes can feel that the relationship is in jeopardy. Ones often feel unsettled when they aren't sure how someone else will respond to them. Sixes can be more reactive and express how they're feeling, which can cause Ones to feel that Sixes aren't seeing things correctly. When this happens, disconnection is possible.

STRENGTHS: Ones and Sixes are both supportive and loyal, so they can build deep trust and long-term commitment.

AREAS TO WORK ON: At times, the desire for predictability can cause strain in the relationship. Individuals grow and change throughout their lives, but if either partner sees self-development as evidence that the other partner isn't true, predictable, or steady, the relationship can suffer. Making time to have fun together and be spontaneous can be a great way to reinforce the idea that things don't always have to be predictable to be connective.

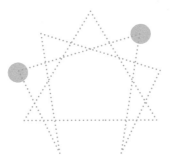

1-7

A One-Seven relationship is the definition of "opposites attract." Both tend to be fairly idealistic. The One sees the ideal world and works for it by doing what is right, being highly responsible, and raising their standards. The Seven, on the other hand, sees that the ideal world exists somewhere in the universe, and they chase it down by staying optimistic, seeking new opportunities, and finding fun in little moments. These differing approaches to idealism can simultaneously attract a One and a Seven or break them apart.

Despite opposing perspectives, these types balance each other. The One helps the Seven be more steady and conscientious, while the Seven helps the One see the ways that everyday life is worth celebrating. Both can get caught up in their own pursuits, so they can help each other see beyond themselves and their path.

The strength of the relationship depends on how each type approaches their differences. The Seven can either feel trapped or steadied by the One's predictability and routine. The One can feel like they are the only adult in the room because of the Seven's tendency to run from pain, or they can feel lightened by seeing shades of gray in their black-and-white perspective.

Sevens and Ones both place a high value on friendship and loyalty—two factors that will help them build a lasting relationship. Sevens are often reluctant to wade into difficult emotions, so loyalty and closeness must be established before they are willing to be vulnerable. Once a Seven feels comfortable and like they can be themselves, there is room for greater depth. Ones look for someone who will continue to show up for them in the relationship, so trust takes time as Ones wait to see if Sevens will be consistent.

STRENGTHS: Both Ones and Sevens can see that a better world can exist, and they can dream together about its potential.

AREAS TO WORK ON: Sevens tend to run from conflict, and Ones can feel abandoned when they feel that Sevens are disengaged. If this dynamic begins, reaffirm your love and care. Assuring and acknowledging each other will help ease some of the tension so conflict can be navigated effectively.

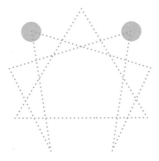

1-8

Ones and Eights are both justice-oriented and fair, and they value truth above all else. Both tend to take responsibility to correct injustice in the world around them, so they can be a powerful couple. The One brings a methodical and intentional approach to life and the relationship, which is comforting for the Eight, who wants things to get done but is more focused on the big picture. The Eight brings self-assurance and an inner drive that can help the One move forward even when their inner critic gets loud.

The Eight is deeply loyal and protective of the relationship and their partner. The One is trustworthy, which helps the Eight feel at peace, knowing they won't be betrayed. These types offer each other much space and autonomy, which both often need. Although less healthy Ones can seem calculated and less healthy Eights can seem tough or angry, a deep tenderness and commitment can build between this couple over time. Knowing each other intimately and emotionally can take time, but both the One and the Eight can feel misunderstood, so feeling mirrored and seen will transform them.

Tension can arise in this couple when they both hold fast to their convictions, but disagree on what those convictions actually are. The often strong-willed One and Eight can dig in their heels, believing their way is right and refusing to acknowledge any gray area.

STRENGTHS: Their admirable shared value of justice, truth, and commitment helps Ones and Eights cultivate a deep, dedicated connection.

AREAS TO WORK ON: The self-controlled One can feel that the intense and direct Eight is being inappropriate, while the Eight can feel that the One is trying to control them. It's important for both types to remind each other that they are on the same team.

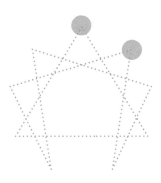

1-9

One and Nine relationships are among the most common Enneagram type pairings. While any relationship can be compatible, it seems that Ones and Nines balance each other particularly well. Both are harmonious, principled, and self-sacrificial. Both truly want peace in the world, but they have different ways of finding it. The One creates peace by working hard, getting things done, and taking care of practical needs. Their consistency, routine, and commitment to the little things creates the peace that the Nine seeks. The Nine in turn tends to create peace by cultivating comfortable physical, mental, or emotional space, and by offering full acceptance to the One. Unhealthier Ones tend to experience a great deal of self-rejection, so feeling complete acceptance from a partner can remind them that they are good, loved, and wanted.

The Nine and the One balance each other similarly in communication. The Nine helps the One value people over principle, while the One helps the Nine to find their voice and use it. In this way, their greatest individual strengths serve them as a couple. Each can feel a sense of underlying purpose and has their own methods of propelling each other toward fulfilling it while remaining ethical and considerate.

Nines and Ones are both in the Gut triad, so their underlying emotion is anger. The One suppresses it, believing it is not "appropriate" to express it, while the Nine forgets their anger and simply falls asleep to it. Tension can lead to passive-aggressiveness, distance, stubbornness, silence, or an explosive argument. Either way, neither type leaves the conflict feeling happy with how it went.

STRENGTHS: Both Ones and Nines kind, communicative, and intentional with the other.

AREAS TO WORK ON: It's important to find healthy ways to deal with conflict early so it doesn't feel so scary later, and to do little things for each other to help each feel loved and known. The Nine could take care of a few practical tasks, while the One could make space for peace, togetherness, and connection (even if they haven't completed their to-do list).

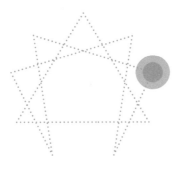

2 - 2

As with all same-type pairings, Twos can be drawn together because they understand each other innately. They are both highly affectionate, kindhearted, and compassionate. Twos often love others in the way they would like to be loved and can feel let down when others don't show up for them. Their love and kindness toward each other is matched and may even be exceeded, which helps each partner feel deeply seen and known.

This pair is generous toward each other and others and gives of themselves to meet others' needs. They are both considerate, caring, passionate, and emotional. They cultivate a deep and reciprocal intimacy because both want the other to feel fully loved and wanted. They can find deep connection quickly due to the comfort and affirmation of being loved.

Accepting help from each other is a challenge for this couple. Twos—especially when less healthy—often believe that they can help others and that they don't need help themselves. A Two can also perceive a rejection of help as a rejection of them as a person. When both parties resist help and feel rejected when their offer to help is refused, this complicates the relationship. It's equally important for both to pause and reflect on motivation before they jump in to help, and learn to accept help when it's offered and they need it. The relationship will flourish if both can learn to have boundaries around when and how to help others and to accept help themselves.

STRENGTHS: Twos long to feel lovable, valued, and cared for; both partners in this relationship specialize in making their partners feel this way.

AREAS TO WORK ON: Twos tend to use most of their energy caring for others and end up with little left for themselves. It can be a challenge for Twos in a relationship to feel permission to care for themselves and focus on their own needs. It might also be difficult for them to articulate their needs to each other, especially if they continually go unmet.

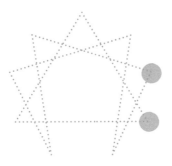

2 - 3

A relationship between a Two and a Three is full of charm, passion, and charisma. Both tend to be engaging and sociable, and their differences complement their similarities. Twos are accepting and encouraging, so their frequent affirmation helps the Three remember that they are loved as they are. This reminds the Three that they don't have to perform to be acceptable to their partner, and they feel more free to express themselves and live fully for who they really are. Threes are encouraging in their own right, and they tend to inspire their partner to appreciate their full potential. The Three's encouragement can help the Two accomplish their big dreams and take time for themselves.

Both of these types crave attention from their partner, but neither is great at asking for it. The Two often finds themselves pouring their energy into the lives of others, while the Three often pours all their energy into the tasks they need to accomplish. When either type focuses solely on these things, the relationship can suffer. It's important to make space to give each other attention, to build the type of connection both desire.

Twos and Threes are skilled at creating strong interpersonal connections, so they can build attraction quickly when they find each other compelling and heartfelt. As the initial attraction fades, their depth, interest, and emotional connection will help the relationship continue to flourish. Together, this pair is dynamic, powerful, and inviting.

Troubles in this relationship are often exacerbated by repeated dynamics. The Three can feel overwhelmed by the Two's helpfulness and desire for emotional connection, while the Two can feel forgotten due to the Three's ambition and task-orientation. Both tend to create busy lives, yet still crave depth in a relationship, so it's important to make space for each other.

STRENGTHS: Twos and Threes encourage and see the value in each other. They deeply desire connection and are good at bringing out the other's better qualities.

AREAS TO WORK ON: While Twos and Threes tend to be aware of what others are feeling, neither is particularly good at identifying their own feelings. Both types can need a little time and thought to pinpoint exactly what is going on inside. Each type should work on feeling their own feelings—not those of their partner—and expressing them. Learning to ask reflective questions will help them draw each other out.

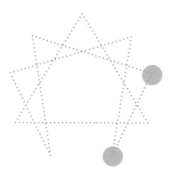

2 - 4

Twos and Fours together are empathetic, intimate, and connected heart-forward types, drawn to each other's emotional intelligence and depth. They crave deep connection and find it together when both are healthy. The Four tends to live inside their heads, but the Two's curiosity and intentional questions help draw them out, so the Four can connect in the world. The Four's curiosity about the Two's internal feelings can help the Two tune in more to their own emotional life. The Four tends to feel inward and the Two outward, so they can each offer what the other lacks.

The typically more sociable Two brings a friendly, generous nature to the relationship, while the Four rounds it out with depth, humor, and creativity. They can build an emotionally fulfilling relationship, especially because they both tend to be wholeheartedly committed.

The Two and Four show up for each other. The Two is often a bit more practical about the daily needs of life, while the Four tends to focus on their mutual emotional, mental, and spiritual health. Such an intense connection can be challenging and even lead to conflict, because they can expect a lot of each other.

The Four often has a stormy internal world. The Two might feel the need to fix the Four's mood, even if it has nothing to do with the relationship, so they don't absorb their negative energy. The Four can feel put off by the Two's desire to fix, and the dynamic can spiral into challenging and sensitive emotional spaces.

STRENGTHS: Twos and Fours complement each other well and offer each other a deep sense of feeling known and wanted.

AREAS TO WORK ON: Both can become absorbed in their partner's emotional world. It's important to practice boundaries so each can maintain an individual identity. The Two can attend to their own needs, and the Four can maintain the independence that they value.

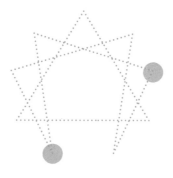

2-5

While Twos and Fives tend to be opposite in many ways, this is one of the more common type combinations. These types are both thoughtful, kind, and fairly accepting, and tend to have an intense attraction because they see in each other what they lack within themselves.

The Two brings a sense of warmth, ease, and comfort to the Five, who typically prefers to keep a quiet distance from the world. The Two can help the Five truly feel their feelings and be more grounded in the present rather than living inside their heads. As the Two draws the Five out, the Five will become increasingly skilled at processing and sharing their emotions. The Five offers the Two a sense of calm and steady objectivity, which can have a similar grounding effect on the Five. Because the Five has strong boundaries, they will often push back on the Two's desires to help, clarifying what truly is the Two's responsibility. The Two can learn over time to ask these questions of themselves. The Five's deep commitment and loyalty can help the Two feel more at home in the relationship.

Part of this pair's attraction is that they find each other mysterious. Twos are relationally and emotionally curious, while Fives tend to be more mentally curious about various ideas. If the latest topic of study is each other, both the Two and the Five can feel deeply fulfilled by the value they offer in the relationship.

A major difference is how each type interacts with feelings. The Five feels their feelings and then detaches from them, so their emotions cannot crowd their mental clarity. The Two, however, spends a good deal of time thinking about their feelings and the feelings of others. This comes naturally to them, and they may feel that the Five is too sterile or detached from the world.

STRENGTHS: The Five appreciates the Two's passion and relational attention, while the Two loves that their Five is endlessly fascinated by them.

AREAS TO WORK ON: Twos tend to be openhearted and optimistic and process outwardly, while Fives are rational and often cynical, and process inwardly. It can be difficult for each to feel truly understood by the other. Improving communication will help both partners feel more seen, known, loved, and understood.

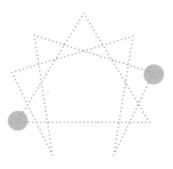

2-6

Twos and Sixes are both incredibly loyal in their relationships. They tend to create a deep bond that can last if both feel safe and wanted. They each crave deep, unwavering connection and will do what is necessary to care for each other well. The Two and the Six both typically attend to practical matters, so neither type feels like they are carrying the full weight of managing daily life.

The Two offers the Six kindness and empathy, especially when the Six worries about possibilities. The Two's supportive listening can help the Six work through their thoughts about a situation and ground them as they consider multiple outcomes. The Six offers the Two thoughtfulness and practicality, helping them feel like they are loved and wanted, since they don't have to pay attention to all the details on their own. Both types are often good at remembering what the other likes and dislikes, so they can help each other feel loved and accepted. The Two's compassion and empathy make the Six feel safe, and the Six's commitment makes the Two feel cherished.

Twos can be highly empathetic, but they also often want to fix what is wrong. It's important for the Six to have space to verbally process anxieties without feeling shut down by their partner. Unfortunately, when the Two tries to fix a problem, the Six can receive the message that it's not okay to speak their mind. This has the unintentional effect of breaking the Six's hard-earned trust, which can strain the relationship. The Six can also be somewhat ambivalent in relationships; sometimes they pull their partner close, and sometimes they push them away. This dynamic can cause the Two—who craves the consistency of a partner who always shows up in the same way—to feel insecure about the status of the relationship.

STRENGTHS: Twos and Sixes often have a truly reciprocal relationship, which is important to both of them. They are good at making time for deep conversation, heart connection, and fun.

AREAS TO WORK ON: Both Twos and Sixes fear rejection and betrayal, so it's important that they find time to talk through their fears rather than shutting down. Both have an instinct to move away when things feel unsure, but it's more productive to lean in.

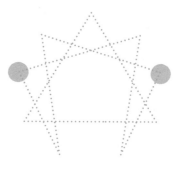

2-7

Twos and Sevens are fun-loving, energetic, and sociable, and both tend to look on the bright side of life. They share an open-hearted and often whimsical view of the world, with light and loving spirits. These traits draw them to each other, and there can be a great deal of excitement and fun in this relationship.

The Seven offers the Two excitement about life and a push to dream bigger, think about possibilities, and look toward the future. The Two is skilled at determining what needs to be done right in front of them and taking action in the present, but they aren't always good at looking to the future. The Seven helps the Two go after their dreams and connect with the potential inside them. The Two helps the Seven see how their actions affect others, and gently nudges them to grow in compassion for others. Sevens are openhearted and can be sensitive, but they don't always delve into more difficult emotional spaces. A Two's care can help the Seven dig deeper and share more emotionally.

There is also a great deal of balance in this pair when it comes to self-care. Sevens are good at looking out for themselves but aren't always aware that they are running themselves into the ground by jumping from one thing to the next. Alternatively, Twos are good at taking care of others, but they aren't always aware that they are wearing themselves out by constantly putting the needs of others before their own. These types can remind each other to take care of themselves in different ways.

Sevens can sometimes feel overwhelmed by the helpfulness and emotional needs of Twos. They tend to reject being trapped or tied down, especially if they aren't sure about the relationship yet. This can cause the Two to fear rejection, and they may dig in and try to be more helpful. This dynamic can spell trouble for the relationship unless they take the time to sit and discuss their differing relational patterns.

STRENGTHS: Both the Two and the Seven love to have fun and be with people, so this can be a great pair with a wide social net.

AREAS TO WORK ON: Conflict can be really challenging for this pair. The Two and the Seven typically both try to stay positive, which can lead to more avoidance of trouble in the relationship. A focus on effective communication will help them both find the love, acceptance, and loyalty that they truly desire.

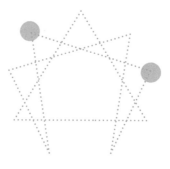

2-8

Twos and Eights tend to have a highly complementary, passionate relationship because—like many of the other "opposite" couples—both tend to offer the other something important that they need. Eights are often drawn to the Twos' gentleness, because they know they need it in their lives and they also want to protect the pure innocence they see in Twos. Twos are often drawn to the power and tenacity of Eights because they admire it and also know they need more Eight energy.

The Eight and the Two are passionate people, but the passion looks different for each of them. The Eight's passion comes out in high volume, strong opinions, and direct communication. The Two's passion often looks like an outpouring of love and depth of care for others. These different brands of intensity can draw them together, especially when they are intentional and generous with others.

It's important for both the Eight and the Two to feel safety and openness in a relationship. If they are not paying attention to their emotions, Twos can begin to feel their partner's feelings rather than their own. If a Two misreads an Eight's passion as anger and assumes it is directed at them, it can strain the relationship significantly. It's important that this pair pay attention to communication and notice this tendency before it gets worse. The Eight, on the other hand, can perceive any shifting in their partner as dishonesty. The Two can have some shape-shifting tendencies, so if they change noticeably, the Eight can have difficulty trusting them. The Eight may begin to pull away if they feel like the Two's love is too much.

STRENGTHS: Twos and Eights can "get" each other on a deep level, simply because they see what they need in each other and respect their individual strengths.

AREAS TO WORK ON: It's really important that these types remain clear, honest, and kind with each other. It can be easy for the Two to feel overwhelmed by the Eight's intensity, and the Eight to feel overwhelmed by the Two's helpfulness. Giving each other the benefit of the doubt will help smooth tensions and pave the way for lasting connection.

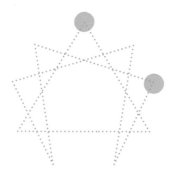

2-9

Twos and Nines in a relationship share many similar values. They are both warm and loving, and want to create a mental, emotional, and physical space full of comfort, harmony, and love. Both want kindness, emotional honesty, acceptance, and good communication in their relationship. They tend to focus on others, which creates plenty of openness and love because each feels known and seen by the other.

Especially when unhealthy, the Two often helps from a place of obligation. The Nine is accepting and undemanding of others, which offers the Two freedom not to be helpful (and the Nine prefers presence over helpfulness anyway). The Nine, on the other hand, is balanced by the Two's relational curiosity. Because they often suppress their own thoughts, ideas, and concerns for fear of disrupting the peace, the Nine can stay silent if their partner isn't willing to truly connect and patiently listen. The Two offers the Nine that peace and patience, because they genuinely want to get to know them on a deeper level.

These types can actually build each other up using these differing strengths, instill more self-confidence, and help each other become more self-aware. It can be difficult for this pair to engage in healthy conflict, however. Both types typically like to look on the bright side and stay positive, but they both care deeply if something is bothering their partner. Therefore, they might be inclined to try to work things out if they are feeling safe and supported. If not, conflict can simmer and devolve into resentment or passive-aggressive swipes at their partner.

STRENGTHS: Twos and Nines both desire peace and positivity, so they will give each other their full attention when they spend time together.

AREAS TO WORK ON: It's crucial that a Two and a Nine work on addressing conflict as it arises. Problems mount as they go unacknowledged, so giving voice to issues can actually help lessen their weight and help the relationship flourish overall. This pair needs to remember that true peace is only accomplished when conflict is attended to in a healthy way.

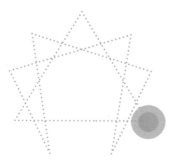

3 - 3

When Threes get together, they create a dynamic, safe, and mutually beneficial relationship. They can be charming, successful, and sociable on their own, yet they tend to have a calming effect on each other in a relationship. It can be incredibly comforting to find a person who understands the desire to shape-shift and perform yet doesn't require it. As with all same-type pairings, two Threes have an ability to understand each other in a way others don't.

Threes are heart-centered types, but they tend to stay busy and work hard to avoid feeling their feelings. As a result, they don't readily share or process emotions outwardly. When two Threes are in a relationship, they understand this and are able to help each other process in a way that other types may not. This mirrored feeling allows both to let down their guard enough to let the other truly see and know them, building intimacy, connection, and awareness. Threes are genuine, loving, and caring in relationships, especially when they feel a sense of mutual trust and respect.

Threes are encouraging and supportive of their partners because they see potential in everyone they meet. Threes can cheer each other on when things aren't going as planned. This can be affirming and steadying for each of them, since they feel safe enough not to perform when they feel supported. Both want to be admired, but underneath the outward pursuit of success is an inner longing to be valued and worthy. When affirmed for who they are, not what they do, Threes can find depth and attachment in their relationship.

The challenge for this pairing is that they can keep themselves so busy that they neglect time to connect and truly get to know each other. It can leave one or both feeling dismissed when one Three doesn't make time or attention for the other. Their penchant for productivity often means they reserve little time for rest, so they need to closely observe this tendency and intentionally make space for downtime.

STRENGTHS: Threes share the same desire for a deep, genuine relationship, productivity, and positivity. They can get along really well because they "get" each other.

AREAS TO WORK ON: Because Threes rarely pause long enough to let their feelings rise, they can easily grow disconnected if they don't take time to emotionally connect. It's important for each partner to understand the importance of true heart-mind integration, so the relationship can be fruitful and connected.

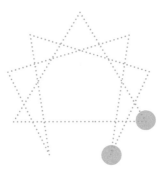

3-4

In a relationship, a Three and a Four are typically intense, communicative, and earnest. They tend to have different energy levels, especially when it comes to processing feelings, but they can bring a great deal of balance to each other that is valuable for each type. The Three is practical and ambitious, so their presence in the Four's life offers structure and confidence, which the Four can sometimes lack. The Three sees the potential in others, so they can help the Four quiet their self-doubt so that they can be more present and action-oriented. The Four is deep and introspective, and curious about their partner's emotional life. Since the Three often struggles to sort out their feelings, a supportive Four can help slow them down, draw them out, and bring attention to their internal life.

Both the Three and the Four can help each other pay attention to the details that truly matter to each of them. Their tendency to be somewhat opposite helps bring balance and reciprocity to the relationship. They can cultivate depth, meaning, and value together as they learn to balance each other.

Both value good communication, although they tend to go about it differently. Specifically, in conflict, Fours tend to say exactly what they are thinking and feeling. It's important that they feel mirrored and seen—never fixed—to reach a resolution. Threes, on the other hand, tend to try to navigate the best way forward without letting too many feelings take them off course. This dynamic can be explosive at times. The Three may feel overwhelmed by the Four's emotional nature and can feel like the Four is being "too much." The Four can see the Three as calculated and will feel dismissed—or, worse, will see the Three as fake. There is nothing more offensive to a Four than a partner who is dismissive or inauthentic. Both need to focus on staying present, listening, and offering each other the emotional space to feel safe and heard.

STRENGTHS: The emphasis both Threes and Fours place on communication is a strength. Both want to feel seen and known, and each partner will do their best to make that happen.

AREAS TO WORK ON: It can be easy in challenging times for this pair to feel like their partner isn't there for them. It's important to communicate expectations and to be aware of unrealistic or unfair demands. Attempting to enforce expectations—such as a certain level of emotional connection or getting things done—will only cause disconnection, and that isn't the goal. They must remember that there is value in their differences.

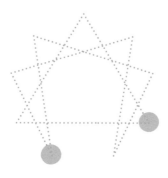

3 - 5

Threes and Fives share the same values of competence and efficiency. Both want to be capable and effective in their specific spheres, and they tend to admire each other's expertise. The Three is typically more sociable, so they offer a sense of poise, energy, and confidence that the Five doesn't display. The Five, on the other hand, is generally more withdrawn, and they offer creativity, depth, and objectivity. The balancing act works well with this pairing because both want to be logical and rational.

When comfortable, both of these types will speak their mind, especially if they are passionate about a topic. This shared communication style can make for interesting and dynamic conversation, and both place a high value on knowing and understanding each other. The Three applies their work ethic and desire to please to the relationship, while the Five tends to research and study their partner as they would any topic they enjoy. The result is a deep connection and knowledge of their partner that is almost hard to explain because it seems to work so seamlessly.

The trouble in this relationship often involves the differing energy levels in each type. The Five has a lower energy threshold in general, and they tend to conserve their energy and then measure it out a bit at a time. Unexpected emotional encounters or social gatherings can feel draining to them. The Three, on the other hand, can seem to have endless energy to accomplish the things they want to do. They don't give much energy to their emotions, but they do spend a great deal of energy being productive and spending time with others. This difference can be troublesome when the Three and the Five simply cannot understand how the other functions.

STRENGTHS: Shared values of kindness and depth can help Threes and Fives create a strong connection, even when their differences are great.

AREAS TO WORK ON: Understanding and giving space to each other is the key. For example, rather than pushing the Five to stay at a party, it's normally best for the Three to take a step back and realize that a Five is asking to leave early because they've reached a personal boundary of how much they can extend themselves—not because they are trying to ruin the Three's time. Fives tend to process their thoughts and feelings inside, while Threes tend to be more verbal processors. The Five can then feel like the Three doesn't make sense, and they can grow frustrated. It's important for the Five to give the Three space to process and to offer kind, listening support.

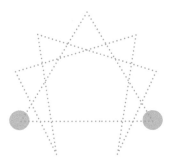

3 - 6

Both Threes and Sixes are committed to causes they believe in and to each other. They are each resilient in their own way, and they apply their attention and work ethic to anything that comes their way. The Three and the Six can share a lot of similar qualities, and they can make a great team.

The Six supports the Three by having an understanding of all the possible outcomes of a situation, so they help tailor and troubleshoot the Three's plans. The Three offers the Six confidence and optimism which the Six sometimes lacks, helping the Six feel more steady. They ground each other; the Six helps the Three slow down a bit and make time for true connection, while the Three helps the Six cut through their swirling thoughts and gain more clarity.

The Six can be more outwardly emotional than the Three, but their typical way of expressing themselves is not too overwhelming for the Three. The Three, on the other hand, can be positive and hopeful, but they aren't blind to negative outcomes, which can validate the Six. This reciprocity tends to work well. The trouble starts when the Six sees the Three's tendency to act as a chameleon. Honesty and loyalty are of the utmost importance for Sixes. If they sense their partner is being anything but 100 percent honest, they may lose trust, and feel unsafe. Threes can read the Six's cautious and questioning nature as a hindrance or, worse, as a lack of belief in the Three and their abilities. If the Three or the Six feels unsafe or unsupported, the relationship can become challenging.

STRENGTHS: Both Threes and Sixes tend to be highly communicative and able to express what they need when they are comfortable. They can cultivate a relationship of healthy interdependence.

AREAS TO WORK ON: Sixes pay attention to caution, while Threes pay attention to ambition. These two focuses seem naturally at odds and can cause challenges to this pairing. It's important that both the Three and the Six validate their respective feelings of caution and ambition, so they can both feel present, safe, and valued in the relationship.

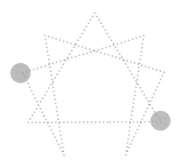

3 - 7

Threes and Sevens both value fun, taking action, and moving forward. They share a common zest for life, and tend to have a great time together. They can be vivacious and adventurous, and provide balance to each other.

The Three tends to be more practical, and can help the Seven be more focused, grounded, and goal-oriented. The Seven is quick-minded, so their thoughts often move quicker than they can. The Three helps the Seven find what they really care about and chase after that one goal, rather than running down every idea that pops into their heads. The Seven tends to be more whimsical, open, and spontaneous—qualities that help the Three see that life is more than just marking things off a to-do list. A Three can let loose and actually celebrate the joy life has to offer with a Seven's influence, rather than feeling the need to earn excitement.

The Seven tends to appreciate the poise and sensitivity the Three brings, while the Three is often impressed by the vast knowledge and fascinating topics the Seven offers. Both like to stay busy and they can be a productive, dynamic pair.

At times, the Three can struggle with the Seven's tendency to get excited about everything. The Three likes to get things done, and they will apply themselves all the way through the end of the project. Threes can feel frustrated by what they see as the Seven's flightiness. The Seven can get frustrated with the Three's focus on efficiency and practicality in every area of life. They see life as so much more than that, and at times they can feel dismissed or trapped by the Three's tendency to give full attention to tasks rather than to the relationship.

STRENGTHS: The Three and the Seven share a lot of the same energy, and they tend to be bold, courageous, and even entrepreneurial. They like to keep things interesting.

AREAS TO WORK ON: In order to have a healthy relationship, this pair will need to pay close attention to their tendency to run from feelings and must slow down enough to actually feel. They both *want* depth and meaning in the relationship, but sometimes might forget that the way to find that is to stop and explore feelings. Emotional connection can deepen and expand the relationship more than adventure ever will.

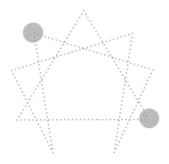

3 - 8

Threes and Eights both tend to be intense, dynamic, and lively in a relationship. They share a sense of passion and assertiveness, and tend to go after what they want in life with full force. Both of these types can get feedback that they are too intense or intimidating for others, so when they are together, they share a mutual appreciation of finding someone who matches their energy.

The Three can help the Eight let go of a bit of their desire for control. The Three's competence and responsibility helps the Eight release themselves from feeling like they have to do everything alone. The Three tends to be more aware of the feelings and needs of others, so they help soften the Eight as they bring attention to areas that the Eight cares about, but doesn't always think about. The Eight gives the Three safety and a space where they don't feel they have to perform. The Eight highly values authenticity, and they aren't impressed when others attempt to show off. Thus, the Three feels comfortable to be who they truly are without pretense.

Communication is a priority for this pair. Both can often rely on intuition to guide them—the Three relies on their emotional intelligence to read the room, and the Eight relies on their gut intuition to tell them who is trustworthy and who isn't. If both types rely heavily on this intuition rather than communicating, the relationship can become troubled because they can sometimes read things incorrectly. It's important that both partners communicate to maintain trust and authenticity in the relationship.

STRENGTHS: Threes and Eights often understand each other well because of their shared energy and intensity. They create a safe harbor for each other.

AREAS TO WORK ON: Industrious, hardworking pairs like this need encouragement to take a night off, rest, and have fun. Threes and Eights need to plug fun dates into their busy schedules to cultivate real emotional connection and let loose a little. Things don't always have to be under control.

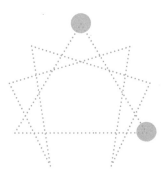

3-9

Threes and Nines make a great pair. They support each other and are purposeful in their lives. Nines are encouraging and supportive partners. They accept and love the Three simply for being who they are, not for what they do, which is a comforting change for the Three who often feels the need to perform for others. The Three bolsters the Nine's confidence and helps them understand and express their desires and motivations.

A Three and a Nine can cultivate a happy, positive relationship because they balance each other so well. The Nine often finds themselves drifting into the background of their own lives, but a supportive Three partner can help bring them back into the light. The Three often finds themselves doing so much that they don't take a break, but a Nine partner can help them take a break from their productivity so that they can recharge.

A Three and a Nine can have conflict over their differing energies. The Three tends to be active and productive, and they can get frustrated by the Nine's tendency to move at a slower, more methodical pace. A frustrated Three can see the Nine's processing time as laziness. The Nine, on the other hand, can feel rushed by the Three's desire to move faster. The Three's intense pace can make the Nine feel that they've been left in the dust.

STRENGTHS: Threes and Nines are both open and communicative in relationships, and they want to talk through things to cultivate a level of trust.

AREAS TO WORK ON: Threes and Nines can both have a tendency to go with the flow in the relationship. While Threes are generally fairly assertive, they want their partner to be happy and will often do whatever is needed to make things feel peaceful and positive. Nines also tend to merge with their partners, so sometimes both Threes and Nines can melt into each other a bit.

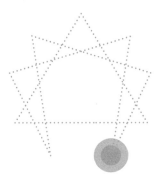

4 - 4

Fours are idealistic, emotional, and empathetic. They are often very expressive and tend to think deeply about their thoughts, feelings, and ideas. Many Fours also feel as deeply as they think and have a broad range of emotional experiences. Fours in a relationship can help each other feel mirrored, known, and seen. Because both know what it's like not to feel these things, they know how to make each other feel truly understood.

Fours can discuss their deepest feelings, dreams, past experiences, and disappointments in great detail. This couple can know each other fully and deeply because they are both so introspective and often quite communicative. However, a Four can never be fully known, because they are always on a quest of self-discovery. This actually keeps things interesting for this couple and can be a great asset to the relationship, especially as they learn, grow, and shift throughout life. Fours tend to fall in love quickly and dive headlong into relationships.

Fours can be reactive, so conflict can be challenging for this couple. They can both say things they don't mean and feel incredibly wounded by their partner's words. It's important for Fours to feel like there is actually safe space between them, not just the pretense of space. Independence is important for a lot of Fours because they need that extra space to sort through their feelings.

STRENGTHS: Fours feel truly understood by each other and can feel a soul-level acknowledgment of each other's significance.

AREAS TO WORK ON: The idealism of Fours means that they not only see the perfect world that could exist, but also long for it and mourn that it does not already exist. This can cause them to focus more on what's missing—both inside them and in the world around them—rather than seeing life in a positive or even realistic way. Practicing gratitude by noticing what's already good and speaking it out loud will help with this.

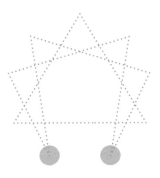

4 - 5

Fours and Fives have a lot in common, which makes this a fairly natural pairing. Both share a desire for depth, understanding, and interesting conversation. The Four and the Five are both fairly introspective and interested in each other's minds. This can help them find the total understanding they are looking for in a significant other.

The Five steadies the Four by remaining objective and rational through life's ups and downs. Their wisdom helps the Four think through their many dreams and ideas. The Four helps the Five rediscover their emotions by reminding them of the beauty and light all around them. This attention to creativity helps the Five honor their feelings without needing to detach from them.

The biggest difference between these two types is how they engage with emotions. The Four feels their feelings completely; rather than dulling their feelings, they often turn the intensity up to understand themselves more fully. The Five feels things, but they detach quickly and opt to look at life with a quiet objectivity. They often feel that getting caught up in emotion will make them less capable or confident, so they intentionally detach to stay objective. This can cause miscommunication in conflict. The Five's objectivity can cause the Four to feel like their partner isn't "in it" with them, while the Four's emotional expression can feel overwhelming to the Five. Good communication can help resolve this dynamic.

STRENGTHS: Both the Four and the Five are inquisitive, curious, and imaginative. They can offer each other a good deal of balance, which helps them both feel more grounded.

AREAS TO WORK ON: Both Fours and Fives can hesitate to take action because they feel the need to process decisions thoroughly before moving forward. The Four relies a bit more on their feelings, while the Five tends to rely almost solely on their mental faculties. It's important for this couple to remember that both thoughts and feelings are needed, and that there is value in moving forward even when things don't feel fully sorted.

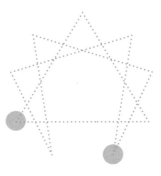

4 - 6

Fours and Sixes tend to be expressive, sensitive, and affection-ate. Both tend to react with their full feelings in the world, which can give them a deep sense of similarity. Because they tire of accusations of being too much or being "hysterical," they tend to avoid such characterizations of each other, and instead seek to be kind and compassionate when their partner expresses how they feel.

It's really important for a Six to feel like their concerns are taken seriously, and a Four—with their ability to empathize without feeling the need to fix it—is a good sounding board. This gives the Six space to feel and to express themselves without the frustration of feeling dismissed. The Four tends to express their dreams and ideas, and their imagination can help the Six see what is possible in a positive way. The Six's practicality grounds the Four, and the Four can feel taken care of by the Six's responsibility and attention to detail. Both are searching for depth in a relationship, and they long to find commitment and someone they can feel truly at home with. If both the Four and the Six feel safe, they can find the true home they both seek.

A Six and a Four share a tendency to revisit and analyze past conversations in their minds to find where things went wrong. This can be dangerous territory for the relationship. It's important for this pair to offer each other affirmation and reassurance; they need to remind each other that they care deeply and want what is the best for them. Regular, effective communication is the key to warding off any trouble.

STRENGTHS: The Four and the Six balance each other well. They make their partner feel safe, secure, and seen in a way that feels like a soul-level attachment.

AREAS TO WORK ON: It's important for both the Four and the Six to pursue their own growth. With self-awareness, they can begin to see when they are analyzing interactions in their minds and highlighting the negative aspects of their conversation. Learning to identify this pattern will help the relationship overall, especially because this pattern and the insecurity many Fours and Sixes experience are intertwined.

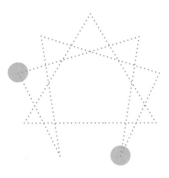

4-7

Fours and Sevens are imaginative idealists. They tend to be quite colorful, expressive, and curious, and want to live life to its fullest. Their penchant for the strange, interesting, and whimsical draws them together, and they often have a magnetic pull toward each other. They like to keep things interesting!

A Seven can help a Four see all the good, joy, and wonder in the world. The Four tends to mourn what's missing, but the Seven balances them by celebrating all the excitement that is already around them in the world. The Seven helps the Four find confidence in themselves because the Seven is truly passionate about all the awesome qualities of the people around them. The Four, on the other hand, helps the Seven stay grounded and create a safe space for the Seven to experience emotions. Sevens don't lack feelings; they just don't often slow down long enough to process them, and they only share them with a few safe people. The Four's willingness to see the dark places can anchor the Seven and welcome them into a fuller expression of life.

A Four and a Seven can overwhelm each other at times. The Four can feel like the Seven's constant motion is too much, and they can feel dismissed and abandoned by the Seven's desire to do anything besides sit in emotional pain. The Seven can feel trapped by the Four's desire for emotional connection, and overwhelmed by the Four's need to express everything fully in the moment. This pairing is fantastic in many ways, but when either partner is unhealthy, they can trigger one another's worst fears.

STRENGTHS: A Four-Seven relationship is never dry or stagnant. They are constantly intrigued and fascinated by each other, and that's one of the many reasons why this works.

AREAS TO WORK ON: It's very important that both Sevens and Fours feel validated in their emotional expression and the way they show up in the relationship. If the Four tries to bring the Seven back to earth or the Seven tries to cheer the Four up when they aren't ready, the results can be disastrous for their connection. Validating each other will help.

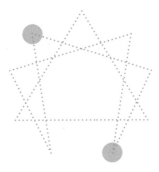

4 - 8

Fours and Eights are passionate, intense, and honest. Authenticity is one of the highest values for both of these types, and this often draws them to each other. This pairing can work really well because they are able to match intensity, but it can also be explosive since both tend to be reactive in conflict.

The Four is sensitive and emotionally vulnerable in a way that the Eight may share but rarely show. The Eight can appreciate the Four's kindness and emotionality because it draws the same out of them. The Eight also may feel compelled to protect the Four at times, which helps the Four feel safe. By contrast, the Eight is practical and tough, and the Four often feels like they need more of that in their lives. There is a sense of give-and-take between these two types as they seem to be simultaneously so similar yet different. The Eight doesn't show many people who they really are, so when they reveal themselves, the Four feels special and important.

There can be a magnetic pull between these two types, since they both tend to like a challenge and enjoy learning the depths of mystery in each other. Both tend to experience visceral reactions to people and situations; the Eight often experiences this as anger, while the Four experiences it as strong emotion in myriad ways. Anger in the Eight can be challenging for a sensitive Four because they tend to internalize it. The Eight's power can be overwhelming for the Four, who tends to be an internal processor. If the Four backs away, it can frustrate the Eight even further since they desire to be on equal footing with their partner.

STRENGTHS: Since both Eights and Fours tend to feel misunderstood by others, they work hard to know each other with authenticity and without assumption.

AREAS TO WORK ON: Because Fours and Eights both tend to be reactionary, a cycle of fighting and making up can feel comfortable. This pattern keeps things interesting, but it's not healthy. It's important for this pair to learn the art of communicating strongly and with passion, without taking things so personally. This often comes with the maturity of knowing when to respond and when to keep quiet.

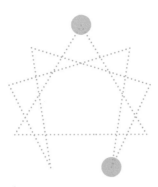

4 - 9

Fours and Nines in a relationship share a common sense of empathy and sensitivity. They are both kind and can be withdrawn, especially when processing their thoughts and feelings. Both the Four and the Nine pursue comfortable emotional and physical spaces, and create that sense of ease and relaxation for each other. They both also prioritize talking through things, although their methods differ.

The Four tends to be highly self-aware, since they spend their lives reflecting on themselves, their identity, and what is happening inside. This self-awareness also causes a curiosity about their partner and can help draw the Nine out. The Four brings emotional awareness to the Nine and helps encourage them to identify and voice their thoughts, preferences, and feelings. The Nine is very accepting, which helps the Four feel secure, since the Four tends to experience a good bit of self-rejection. Nines are more pragmatic, and their steadiness is grounding for Fours, who can be a bit all over the map. Both types tend to be withdrawn, but together they can actually help encourage each other to be more engaged in the present.

A Four and a Nine both appreciate good communication, but they often differ in the way they engage with each other. The Nine can feel overwhelmed by the strong emotions that the Four tends to express. It can throw off their equilibrium to the point that it deeply unsettles them. The Four wants depth and emotional honesty, so when the Nine withdraws, it can make them feel like the Nine isn't really with them in whatever they're experiencing. It's okay for either type to feel the way they do, but they need to strike the balance of withdrawal and expression. Reassurance will go a long way to help each other feel safe and secure.

STRENGTHS: Fours and Nines share a longing to be fully known, and they can find a deep level of reciprocity and comfort in their relationship.

AREAS TO WORK ON: Since Fours and Nines have some challenging communication patterns, things can go unsaid between them, and this ambiguity can cause the Nine to disengage and the Four to feel that their partner isn't honest. Learning to use words and communicate well will build a more meaningful connection. Writing things down will also help, since both Fours and Nines need ample time to process.

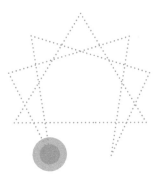

5 - 5

As with any double-type pairing, this pair can be a case of same-strengths, same-weaknesses. Fives share objectivity, wisdom, and intellect. They are cerebral and like to research their favorite topics. Fives enjoy thought-provoking conversations, which can be one of the reasons they are drawn to each other. Most Fives have a few niche interests that they are complete experts in, so when Fives are together, it can be exciting to learn about the other's favorite interests. They enjoy sharing knowledge and thinking through things independently.

Fives generally give each other plenty of space, because they place a high value on personal boundaries. Neither overwhelms the other with demands, since they both are intensely private and avoid intrusion. Fives in general only share when they are fully ready, so when they speak, their thoughts—like paragraphs—have a beginning, middle, and end. It can be frustrating for Fives to be interrupted, so understanding this about each other helps two Fives listen carefully and learn thoughtfully without interrupting their partner. Fives also tend to make witty comments under their breath, and have dark, sardonic humor. Their under-the-radar jokes draw them together and they form a mutual bond.

When two Fives are in a relationship, the biggest challenge is that they have such strong boundaries and independence that they can go days or weeks without emotionally connecting. It's not because the relationship doesn't matter; in fact, Fives are deeply loyal and committed once they are in a devoted partnership. Instead, it's because they find themselves absorbed in research, in their own minds, or doing the things that seem most important to them. If neither partner reaches out, they can grow apart due to complacency.

STRENGTHS: Fives share a sense of methodical decision-making, and deep generosity and kindness toward each other. Feeling known can help them get out of their heads.

AREAS TO WORK ON: Fives tend to see communication—and thereby relationships—as puzzles to be figured out, especially in conflict. When this happens, it's easy to forget that people are not puzzles, but human beings with thoughts and feelings. Engaging with more emotional honesty will actually help this couple develop truer emotional connection and depth in the relationship. The safety they seek is often beneath their emotional boundaries.

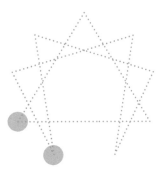

5 - 6

Fives and Sixes share the same values of loyalty and steadiness in a relationship. They enjoy predictability, and offer structure and trustworthiness to each other, which can really help this relationship flourish.

The Six is stabilized by the Five's careful research, knowing that they can rely on the Five to understand necessary details. Both are cautious, but the Six is more action-oriented, which balances out the Five's reluctance to make moves. The Six helps the Five stay connected by showing up as a loyal, committed partner, offering the Five the steadiness and trust they seek as they move deeper into the relationship. Thoughtfulness and attentiveness flow mutually between this pair. While both can experience analysis paralysis, they are better together than separately in terms of making firm decisions.

The differing relationships a Five and a Six have with rules and procedures can pose challenges. Both tend to like systems and practicality, but the Five often rebels against tradition, and question authority on virtually any topic in life. The Six has an ambivalent relationship with authority. Sometimes they are drawn to strong authority and work well within existing systems, while at other times their distrust in authority can cause rebellion. These differing reactions can cause tension, especially when the Five's research and rebellious thinking leads them down a different road than does the Six's careful attention to authority. When the Six doesn't trust the Five's research, the Five can feel deeply hurt.

STRENGTHS: Both Sixes and Fives are witty and clever. They can have fun together, especially when they take time to involve each other in their interests.

AREAS TO WORK ON: The Six needs reassurance that things are going well, and they fear for the health of the relationship when the Five withdraws. The Five withdraws for many reasons—most of them unrelated to the relationship—so they can be confused by the Six's concern about the relationship and request for affirmation. Keeping lines of communication open helps both partners feel safe and committed.

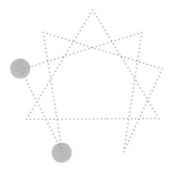

5-7

Fives and Sevens are quick-minded, whimsical, and cerebral. They share a similar desire for thought-provoking conversation, so although they seem very different, they can make a great pair. They are both in the Head triad, so they take in information through their mental faculties. Their minds are constantly moving, and they share a deep sense of fear that they want to understand and escape. They also share values of loyalty and trust in a relationship.

The Five tends to be more grounded, slower moving, and thoughtful. They help the Seven calm down and focus on what they really care about. Their observations and awareness of the world can be an asset to the more erratic Seven, who helps the Five get out of their head and into real life. A Five can find value in the Seven's fresh ideas, spontaneity, and perspective. These types share a similar focus on thinking, but they have vastly different energies and perspectives.

A Five and a Seven both work hard to meet their own needs when stressed. The Five withdraws and finds balance in self-reliance, while the Seven runs headlong into the future. Fives meet their needs by desiring less, while Sevens chase more. They can misunderstand each other, because they meet their similar need for stability in such different ways.

STRENGTHS: Sevens offer fun and excitement, while Fives bring knowledge. They both love anything interesting and enjoy investigating and learning about hobbies and each other.

AREAS TO WORK ON: It's important for this pair to pay attention to each other, not just to their own needs, in stressful times. When they focus on each other, they can learn something valuable from their different approaches to life. They will find more of the contentment and balance they seek if they borrow the other's traits.

5 - 8

Fives and Eights each desire autonomy, loyalty, and trust in a relationship. They are quite independent, and prioritize personal boundaries. In my experience, many early Enneagram learners find multiple similarities on paper between Fives and Eights, but in real life these types have opposite energies. The Five conserves their energy, doling out bits at a time. As one of the most energetic Enneagram types, the Eight tends to express this energy in everything they do. Both types can feel misunderstood by others around them, yet find a deep understanding in each other.

The Five reminds the Eight that fastest is not always best, as a slow and methodical approach almost always trumps brute force for Fives. A Five's steady presence can show an Eight the value in pacing themselves, stepping back, and considering their actions before jumping in. The Eight helps the Five get in touch with their bodies, their intuition, and their basic needs. The Five tends to deny themselves their physical needs because they would rather spend time attending to their minds. Body-oriented Eights help Fives see their power and the gift of their own intuition.

These types demand little of each other aside from loyalty and independence. They can be resistant to trust and the relationship can be slow to grow due to their strong boundaries. They build their independence and self-reliance differently, which can challenge the relationship as they build boundaries around themselves, and not necessarily around their partnership. It's important for this couple to integrate, cultivating a healthy level of dependence and the loving, committed, genuine relationship they both desire.

STRENGTHS: The Five's careful research and the Eight's strength and protection combine to create a feeling of loving safety for each type.

AREAS TO WORK ON: Both the Five and the Eight crave vulnerability in the relationship once they feel safe, yet they also fear it. Neither type likes to admit their own needs, but expressing them will often be an important source of the interdependence of a healthy relationship. Sharing what they need allows this couple to show up for each other and cultivate an emotional connection.

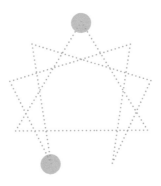

5 - 9

Fives and Nines are thoughtful, accepting, patient, and kind. They are both fairly independent, so this relationship can work well since neither expects too much of the other. Both types can find themselves overwhelmed by the demands of the world, which can be challenging since they each can withdraw when pushed. Neither likes external pressure.

A Nine and a Five have a calming effect on each other. The Five invites the Nine to be more self-expressive, since the Five is quite curious and tends to study a partner as they would any topic of interest. This curiosity can help draw the Nine out and show them it's okay to express themselves and state their needs. The Nine is skilled at making others feel comfortable, so they offer the Five that acceptance and a sense of ease in the world. The Five tends to feel like they can't be fully comfortable in the world, so the Nine helps them to feel more relaxed and at home in their physical space. Both offer each other self-awareness and connection.

The challenge between these types often involves their reactions to conflict. The Nine tends to stay positive and look on the bright side during difficult times to avoid conflict. A Five steps back and analyzes conflict, seeing it as a puzzle to solve. These opposing approaches won't necessarily devolve into an explosive confrontation, but they can give a sense of chasing each other without ever fully dealing with the conflict. Both types value strong communication, so the issues can eventually get worked out once each partner has time and space to process how they feel. Just like the Four and the Nine pairing, a Five and a Nine can benefit by writing down their thoughts and feelings in the midst of conflict.

STRENGTHS: Both Fives and Nines find the comfort they desire in the calm, soothing steadiness of this pairing.

AREAS TO WORK ON: When Fives and Nines seem stuck in communication, it's helpful to do something active, like taking a walk or doing some breathwork. The sensation of feeling the body can be healing and bring some release. Both Fives and Nines tend to have less energy than other types, so getting active can be a challenge, but it helps them to feel the full integration they both want in the relationship.

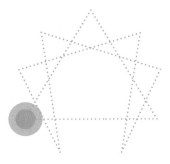

6 - 6

Sixes in a relationship can be best friends. They both desire safety, guidance, commitment, and trust, and they can find these things in each other. Honesty is the most important quality for both of them, and remembering that they share this desire can be reassuring. This relationship can be especially slow to grow since Sixes need a lot of proof before they fully trust someone. That's why Six and Six relationships are often such deep friendships; the romance can only come out of that type of depth.

Sixes together can relax and have fun because they know they have each other's backs. They can talk things through because they place a high value on good communication, enjoy each other's wit, and cultivate deep trust, sensitivity, emotional connection, and love. Sixes are devoted people who can create the life of predictability, consistency, and connection they both crave.

When Sixes are together, they can let their mutual worst-case scenario fears spiral. They can also deeply validate each other—a valuable and reassuring tool when fears run out of control. Their biggest challenge can be difficulty planning, as they tend to struggle with decision-making, especially if they are both trying to determine possible outcomes. As Sixes learn to trust themselves, their decision-making difficulty will lessen.

STRENGTHS: Sixes are compassionate and kind, witty, relational, and connective. They are mutually supportive, which can help them feel reassured in their relationship.

AREAS TO WORK ON: It's important for all Sixes to learn to trust themselves rather than relying on others for reassurance. This is even more true in a relationship between two Sixes. Reassurance and loyalty can help, but Sixes need to learn to notice when they are struggling to see their value, and connect back to their own power.

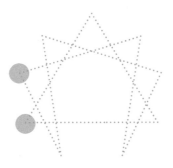

6-7

Sixes and Sevens in a relationship are adventurous best buddies, and truly dynamic together. They seem opposite in many ways, but they both want fun, connection, lightness, and loyalty in their relationship. They are spirited and enthusiastic. The Six tends to be a bit calmer, and this energy stabilizes the Seven, who often has so much energy that they don't know what to do with it.

The Six's stability and caution balance the Seven's enthusiasm. The Seven might seem annoyed with the Six's thoughtful caution at times, but both types share underlying anxiety, and the Seven ultimately appreciates that someone is looking out for them. The Seven helps the Six get out of their head a bit and have some fun; their light spirit offers the Six a sense of courage and confidence that Sixes sometimes lack.

Both the Six and the Seven have fear and anxiety, but they deal with it differently. The Six copes by planning ahead and understanding all the possibilities so they can decide how to proceed. The Seven runs from any negative emotion into the next opportunity. This dynamic can be challenging as it pulls this pair in opposite directions. The Six craves predictability, and the only thing predictable about the Seven is their unpredictability. The Seven can view the Six as negative, and dismiss the Six's concerns as silliness.

STRENGTHS: Sixes and Sevens share a deep desire for friendship and loyalty. When close and healthy, this pair can seem like a troublemaker and a sidekick.

AREAS TO WORK ON: It's important for Sevens and Sixes to communicate well and to respect the different ways they express themselves. Neither will feel safe in the relationship if they feel dismissed or controlled, so opening up to listening and kindness will help cultivate mutual compassion and togetherness.

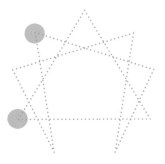

6 - 8

Sixes and Eights can be a fairly natural pairing since each offers something that the other lacks. Both are deeply loyal and tend to like direct communication so that they can get everything on the table. There are typically no secrets in this relationship, and if they exist, they are destructive if discovered. Trust and honesty are the top priorities for this couple.

The Six craves guidance and security, and the Eight offers the protection, strength, and safety the Six seeks. The Six finally feels safe and at home with the Eight, and knowing they can depend on their Eight for anything they need can help calm their fears. The Eight values the Six's honesty and careful thoughtfulness. Sixes are generally warm, devoted, and kind, and Eights—who don't often express their needs—need this. Feeling seen and known by a Six encourages an Eight to be vulnerable in ways that they often hide. The Eight appreciates someone who is consistent and dependable, and they find this in the Six.

The main challenge here is that any breach of trust can be disastrous for the relationship. Betrayal is the worst possible outcome for both of these types, and even "small" lies can feel like betrayal. A Six's typical avoidance of confrontation can feel like dishonesty to the Eight. Overreactions from the Eight can overwhelm the Six, who typically struggles with unpredictability. The Six can be highly reactive as well, so confrontation can be explosive.

STRENGTHS: A Six and an Eight share a high level of reciprocity, honesty, and trust. These aspects of their relationship will have them both in it for the long haul.

AREAS TO WORK ON: It's really important for both Sixes and Eights to remind each other that they are on the same team. Alienation won't help their communication—instead, a deeper connection is the key to combat any of the distance created by cycles of reactivity and conflict avoidance. Both need to remember that not every thought needs to be immediately expressed. Discernment will help calm conflicts and smooth communication.

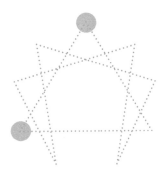

6-9

A Six and a Nine pairing is fairly common. They both offer comfort, stability, connection, and love, and want clear communication, although both can also shy away from it at times. When they feel accepted and open, with a calm, caring space between them, both the Six and the Nine can appreciate the conscientiousness the other brings, and they will be highly invested in the relationship. Togetherness often feels comforting for a Six and a Nine, so they can build a strong reciprocal connection.

The Nine offers the Six a sense of steadying calm. The Nine tends to be slightly detached, so they can listen to the Six discuss their fears and concerns without also getting worried about them. The Nine allows the Six the space they need to process their ideas and come out on the other side with more calm energy and less anxiety. The Six brings devotion and structure to the relationship. A Nine can often float passively through life, but the Six challenges them to think about what they really want in a kind and loving way. The Six is more action-oriented, balancing the Nine's calm energy.

The challenge for types Six and Nine is that both tend to defer to others to make decisions for them. They can make their own decisions, but they like to have input before moving forward, so a Six and a Nine can have trouble deciding how to proceed. Fortunately, they like to talk things through so they can find the best path forward. Their differing levels of independence are another challenge. The Nine is typically a bit more independent, so the Six's desire for connection can cause them to feel overwhelmed. It's important to maintain open communication about this to ensure that both are getting their needs met.

STRENGTHS: Sixes and Nines can cultivate a deep level of friendship because of how they balance each other, and they offer each other unity, affection, mutual support, and healthy interdependence.

AREAS TO WORK ON: Both the Six and the Nine tend to be very supportive of each other, yet both tend to be a bit indecisive. Becoming more clear on what they actually want in life can help the Six and the Nine grow in confidence in themselves and in the relationship.

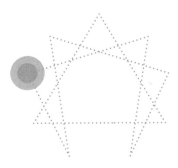

7-7

Sevens are enthusiastic, lighthearted, and appealing. They have a reputation for being flighty or noncommittal, but they simply have broad interests and quick minds. They see opportunity wherever they go, and they are always up for a new challenge, new adventure, or even a new topic to learn about. Two Sevens want to be satisfied and content, and to make each other happy.

Sevens want loyalty and commitment, yet it can take them a while to feel truly safe in relationships. Sevens in a relationship can understand each other's reluctance to go into emotional depth and can challenge each other to be more vulnerable. Healthy Sevens can find a good balance of depth and fun. They are full of grand—sometimes zany—ideas, and often love bouncing them off their partner. Other types could call them unrealistic, but another Seven is along for the ride.

Conflict can really challenge this couple since both like to stay positive, and neither wants to get stuck in negativity. Some Sevens resist conflict since they don't want to deal with difficult feelings, but reaching the contentment both desire sometimes requires wading through the difficult stuff. Practicing vulnerability and affirmation will help this couple deal with conflict so they can find the joy and peace they want.

STRENGTHS: A deep understanding between Sevens helps this relationship thrive. Both partners want independence, and to have a fun, adventurous, and resilient relationship.

AREAS TO WORK ON: Sevens can be really good for each other, but they can also have some challenges. Sometimes Sevens don't realize that they are exhausting themselves by always seeking the next thing. This couple can find more balance and fulfillment by reminding each other it's okay to slow down, pause, and let life unfold.

7-8

A Seven and an Eight relationship is dynamic, captivating, and intense. Both tend to run full speed into life, and they want to get the most they possibly can out of it together. They can actually have a calming effect on each other, since their mutual energy reassures them that they won't feel stuck. Both types tend to be energetic and love excitement, so they can find each other intriguing and challenging.

The Seven brings excitement and fun to the relationship. The Eight can be somewhat serious, so a Seven can help them lighten up and have a good time. Most Eights also have a strong desire for control, but they can't control a Seven, nor can they predict what a Seven will do next. The Eight helps the Seven focus their attention on what truly matters to them, and they are able to help the Seven stay rooted in reality.

The challenge in this partnership is often the way they deal with feelings. Neither really likes to share vulnerability, but the Eight is typically more engaged with their emotions on a regular basis. The Eight doesn't necessarily like conflict, but they can broach difficult topics because they prefer to work through them than to ignore them. The Seven likes to stay positive and doesn't want to feel trapped in frustration or anger. Both types can be fairly sensitive, but they don't normally share that with others. Thus, the Seven can feel hurt or scared by the Eight's anger, and the Eight can feel dismissed by the Seven's desire to keep things light. Good communication and affirmation are necessary to help this couple work together.

STRENGTHS: The Seven and the Eight share excitement for life and a desire to get the most they can from it.

AREAS TO WORK ON: It's important for this couple to slow down a bit and be present with their feelings. Emotional depth can be challenging for them, but it's necessary to create the relationship both the Seven and the Eight truly desire. Pausing to notice reactions will help this pair identify what natural patterns are helping or hurting their relationship. They can find true connection only after working through their individual resistance to their emotions.

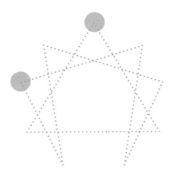

7-9

Sevens and Nines find balance and positivity in a relationship. They see in each other something they each lack, which contributes to their deep connection. Both tend to be carefree, optimistic, and flexible, which draws them to each other. It's important for both a Seven and a Nine to maintain a level of independence while still finding a good deal of time for fun and connection.

The Seven is more assertive than the Nine, and also tends to be more confident and action-oriented. They lend these qualities to the Nine in a relationship, helping them to see their own value and to believe in themselves. The Nine brings a calm, steady energy to the Seven, and they tend to be more emotionally available. This helps the Seven be more engaged, present, and personal. Nines like the status quo, so they are generally content with the way things are. Sevens like to keep things interesting and dynamic. Together, they get what they need.

The Seven finds more peace and contentment, while the Nine finds more variety and interest.

Neither the Seven nor the Nine enjoys conflict. They would rather look on the bright side and stay positive, but both can acknowledge when working through a challenge is necessary to return to a calm and happy place. Both need affirmation that the relationship is not in jeopardy before they are able to participate in conflict resolution. They each crave this reassurance, so they can give it, and trust each other.

STRENGTHS: Sevens and Nines tend to share an accepting, nonjudgmental spirit, which can be comforting for both of them.

AREAS TO WORK ON: Neither the Seven nor the Nine likes to be told what to do. Both can be quite stubborn when they feel pressure from others, and they may react out of frustration by being passive-aggressive or rebellious. The Seven and the Nine do not need to be told what to do, but they do need to be open to feedback, and remember that the other has the best intentions.

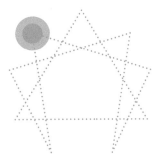

8 - 8

There's never a dull moment in a relationship between two Eights. Both are passionate, protective, energetic, compelling, strong-willed, and powerful. However, they can actually often calm each other and help their partner to relax. There can be a deep level of security in this relationship because they share the value of trust and both avoid being controlled. Knowing that their partner values trust so highly can help an Eight be more at peace and feel more safe.

Eights are typically fairly straightforward in communication, and there is a great deal of comfort in that. The mutuality of love, respect, and appreciation makes each partner feel safe. Eights generally feel the need to be autonomous, and often avoid relying on others. In a relationship with another Eight, they can trust their partner to be as authentic, engaged, invested, and responsible as they are.

Eights are reactive in conflict, which means they want to get all their feelings and thoughts on the table immediately in a confrontation. This can sometimes be helpful because it feels honest and forthright, but when it incites further frustration, it can be challenging. Both Eights can be contrarian, which can cause arguments because they feel like their partner is always contradicting them. It's important for this pair to stay engaged and thoughtful in communication to avoid this.

STRENGTHS: Two Eights share a deep devotion to the relationship and commitment to each other. They are all-in.

AREAS TO WORK ON: Affirming each other can feel vulnerable at times, but it's so important. Eights perceive flattery as manipulation, so they can see right through a fake compliment. They still want to feel appreciated, however, so genuine, kind, specific compliments make a positive difference.

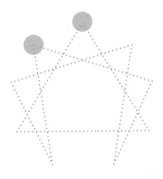

8-9

Eights and Nines share a similar level of devotion and earnestness in a relationship. They can be very intentional, and value fairness, justice, and respect. Eights and Nines work well together because they each offer something the other lacks. As body-centered types, Eights and Nines seek comfort, so they will work hard in a relationship to create a comfortable and peaceful physical, mental, and emotional space for both of them.

The Eight is future-oriented and assertive. They see potential in their partner, and work to inspire confidence and action in the Nine, who tends to be less active. The Eight's encouragement can help the Nine find their voice and realize that it is okay to assert themselves. The Nine often fears that they don't matter in the world, but the Eight's attention can help them see how much they are loved and appreciated. The Nine is accepting and understanding. They see all sides of issues before they engage, and they can help the Eight learn when to pause before reacting so that they can take the right step forward. The Nine also helps the Eight relax a bit, so that they aren't always driving forward at full force. They enjoy the connection and companionship they find in each other.

The biggest trouble spot for this couple is often communication. Their communication styles are so different that they can misunderstand each other, which causes conflict because they are simply missing their partner's perspective. The Eight can be direct, confrontational, and unafraid to get to the point. The Eight isn't necessarily looking for conflict, but they don't shy away from it, especially if they feel that it is necessary to clear the air. The Nine, however, tends to have a much harder time approaching conflict, and they can be easily overwhelmed by the Eight's intensity.

STRENGTHS: Eights and Nines can have a good balance when they are communicating and caring for each other well.

AREAS TO WORK ON: Their differing energy levels need to be managed from both sides. The Eight needs to realize when their manner of speaking is upsetting the Nine and allow their partner the space to process. The Nine needs to notice when the Eight is simply sharing and isn't angry. Giving each other the benefit of the doubt will really help ease communication.

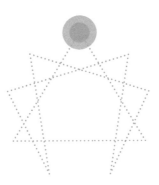

9 - 9

Two Nines in a relationship are connected, harmonious, and serene. They are able to create the balance and companionship together that they seek in their lives. They tend to get along well because neither places high expectations on the other, so they each feel free to live their lives somewhat independently. They enjoy routine and predictability, so they can create patterns that work for them and feel comfortable.

Nines offer each other consistency, warmth, and care. They tend to invite each other to deepen the relationship, but they aren't intrusive or demanding about it. Nines generally like to talk through things, and the same is true in this pairing. They know they each need time to process, so they give each other plenty of space and do not rush their partner into making decisions. They can communicate well because they share a deep understanding of each other, and each accepts the other as they are.

Trouble can arise when Nines withdraw from the relationship because neither is action-oriented, and both tend to be conflict avoidant. If grievances mount on either side and the space between them goes quiet, it can be hard to reignite the relationship because it takes a lot for a Nine to initiate pursuit of the other. The dynamic can grow distant, passive-aggressive, or even silent. Their conflict-avoidant tendencies can get the best of them, and they may disengage.

STRENGTHS: Two Nines create comfort and space for each other, so both are drawn in and feel cozy, warm, and relaxed.

AREAS TO WORK ON: True peace often requires thorough communication and even conflict. Because Nines desire peace, they sometimes avoid talking about the hard things, especially if they aren't sure how they really feel about something yet. Space is okay, but waiting too long to address conflict can actually make it harder to bring it up. Double Nine pairings are typically very patient with each other, so applying that patience to conflict and learning how to work through it together will really help.

RESOURCES

Tests

I've described my distrust of tests in detail, but because I know you'll ask, I'll provide a few good tests to take. Keep in mind that as you learn more about yourself, you might find that your Enneagram type does not line up exactly with your test results. Remember that you can trust yourself and understand your core motivation at a deeper level than any test can. Also, while tests can point you in the right direction, the top two scores are not your core type and wing. As mentioned in the first section of this book, your wing is a type adjacent to your core type that modifies your behavior—essentially how your core motivation is worked out. There is no test to determine your wing. Instead, I recommend noticing how you feel and behave in the world and observing which wing type you relate to most. If you would really like to take a test, I recommend hiring an Enneagram professional to interpret your results.

ENNEAAPP

The EnneaApp (available in the Apple App store and Google Play) is a mobile app full of great Enneagram content. The app is free, but it offers in-app purchases to unlock more tools. You can find your type, learn helpful tips around the Enneagram, and discover more about the Enneagram tool by using this app. Overall, it's a useful tool for Enneagram lovers of all levels. enneaapp.com

This is a classic test for a reason. The Riso-Hudson Enneagram Type Indicator (RHETI) gives scores across all nine types, and also points to a probable core type. It is 144 questions long, and independently scientifically validated (The Enneagram Institute, 2019). This test is of great value to those just starting out with the Enneagram, or those planning on hiring a professional. It can be found on the Enneagram Institute Website. enneagraminstitute.com/rheti

This is perhaps the best and most thorough test, although it is among the most expensive. The iEQ9 is notable in that the test is dynamic; as a participant moves through the assessment, the questions become more tailored to further narrow down the type (Integrative9 Enneagram Solutions, 2020). This can help parse through the differences between various types. This test also identifies the participant's primary subtype. integrative9.com/GetYourType

Books

These books have been beneficial on my personal Enneagram journey. I've read them cover to cover multiple times and return to them to gain deeper insight. I hope you'll find them useful as well.

The Road Back to You: An Enneagram Journey to Self-Discovery by Ian Morgan Cron and Suzanne Stabile

If you've been introduced to the Enneagram in the last few years, you've likely read this book. *The Road Back to You* is a great introduction to the Enneagram system, offering illustrative descriptions of each type.

The Sacred Enneagram: Finding Your Unique Path to Spiritual Growth, by Christopher Heuertz

Heuertz's approach to the Enneagram is a bit of a departure from Cron and Stabile's, but it has great value. This book is deeply spiritual, exploring the Enneagram through a more philosophical lens. It's a great read, full of deep insight and fresh understanding of Enneagram wisdom.

The Wisdom of the Enneagram: The Complete Guide to Psychological and Spiritual Growth for the Nine Personality Types by Don Richard Riso and Russ Hudson

If I could have only one Enneagram book, it would be this one. It's more than 20 years old, but feels every bit as relevant and contemporary as any other Enneagram book I've read. Riso and Hudson present detailed descriptions of every aspect of the Enneagram, and they also dedicate the final section to the specific paths toward growth for each type. I continually glean new insight from this book.

The Complete Enneagram: 27 Paths to Greater Self-Knowledge by Beatrice Chestnut

Chestnut's clear understanding and description of the 27 subtypes is renowned in the Enneagram community for both accuracy and ease of explanation. This book is among the more advanced of the Enneagram books, and it leaves readers feeling like they are getting a master's degree in the topic.

The 9 Types of Leadership: Mastering the Art of People in the 21st Century Workplace, by Beatrice Chestnut

This book is perfect for those in business and entrepreneurship. Chestnut weaves in interviews from some of Silicon Valley's top executives, describing how each of the nine types can be an effective leader. This book is also excellent for those who would like to understand subtypes but feel intimidated by the size and scope of Chestnut's *The Complete Enneagram*.

NOTE: This list is ever-expanding as more and more Enneagram books become available.

Websites

The internet contains endless resources to help you learn more about the Enneagram. Even public forums, like Reddit, can be excellent sources of information. I appreciate the following websites for researching more about each of the nine types.

enneagraminstitute.com

The Enneagram Institute is a great free resource when first learning the Enneagram. The site offers a detailed overview of the Enneagram system, descriptions of each of the nine types, and it even includes common type confusions and how to truly boil it down to one clear type.

theenneagramatwork.com

Peter O'Hanrahan's "The Enneagram at Work" offers a succinct overview of each of the nine types as well as detailed descriptions of how each shows up at work. It's a great resource for those who are seeking slightly more conversational language than is found on The Enneagram Institute's website.

drdaviddaniels.com

Dr. David Daniels, MD, created this website to marry his experience as a psychiatrist with the wisdom of the Enneagram. Writings by the late Dr. Daniels offer fascinating insights on a variety of Enneagram-related topics, including neurobiology and relationships. His perspective was unique because of his background, so his website remains a valuable tool for further growth.

instagram.com/ninetypesco

ninetypes.co

I can be found on Instagram at @ninetypesco or via my website, where you'll find thoughtful and informative content about each Enneagram type as well as the Enneagram system overall.

REFERENCES

Chestnut, Beatrice. *The Complete Enneagram: 27 Paths to Greater Self-Knowledge.* Berkeley, CA: She Writes Press, 2013.

Cron, Ian Morgan and Suzanne Stabile. *The Road Back to You: An Enneagram Journey to Self-Discovery.* Downers Grove, IL: InterVarsity Press, 2016.

Heuertz, Christopher L. *The Sacred Enneagram: Finding Your Unique Path to Spiritual Growth.* Grand Rapids, MI: Zondervan, 2017.

Integrative9 Enneagram Solutions. *The Integrative Enneagram Questionnaire (iEQ9).* Accessed January 29, 2020. https://www.integrative9.com/ieq9products /ieq9-questionnaire

Palmer, Helen. *The Enneagram: Understanding Yourself and the Others in Your Life.* New York, New York: HarperCollins, 1991.

Riso, Don Richard and Russ Hudson. *The Wisdom of the Enneagram: The Complete Guide to Psychological and Spiritual Growth for the Nine Personality Types.* New York, New York: Bantam Books, 1999.

Stabile, Susan and Joel Stabile. (2019, March 8). "Episode 50: Orientation to Time." *The Enneagram Journey Podcast*. [Audio podcast]. Accessed January 29, 2020. https://www.theenneagramjourney.org /podcast/2019/episode50

The Enneagram Institute. *The Riso-Hudson Enneagram Type Indicator (RHETI® version 2.5)*. Accessed January 29, 2020. https://www.enneagraminstitute.com/rheti

INDEX

W

ACKNOWLEDGMENTS

Writing a book has been a lifelong goal for me, and I'm grateful to Rockridge Press for reaching out and initiating this process. I'm honored to be here, and I'm hopeful that this book becomes a guidepost for many on their own journeys of self-discovery. Thank you to those who have been on the team and made this book happen.

Many Enneagram scholars have paved the way for me, and I am forever grateful for their contributions to the ever-evolving ancient wisdom in these pages. The Enneagram's complexity is challenging to capture, yet I've learned so much from the way many authors and teachers have understood and described this tool. I'd like to thank Don Riso, Russ Hudson, Suzanne Stabile, Chris Heuertz, and Beatrice Chestnut, as all of their work has significantly impacted my own path of using the Enneagram. I'd also like to thank my friends, Amanda Steed and Kristi Rowles, who have become both business partners my teachers of the Enneagram.

I am forever grateful to those who participated in my surveys, Instagram stories, and other informal data collection over the last year! I feel honored that you continue to generously share your experiences with such vulnerability and openness.

Finally, I'd like to thank my family. To my steadfast husband, Brandon, thank you for introducing me to the Enneagram years ago, and for cheering me on as I turned a spark of interest into a full-fledged business. Thank you to my parents, Alan and Christin, and my in-laws, Rick and Miranda. Your collective encouragement, enthusiasm, and generosity have always provided me with a soft place to land and the courage to find new heights.